Wo...
for Windows
VisiRef

Ron Holmes

Elden Nelson

Word 6 for Windows VisiRef

Library of Congress Catalog No: 94-65332

ISBN: 1-56529-740-7

96   95   94   6   5   4   3   2   1

Interpretation of the printing code: the rightmost double-digit number is the year of the book's printing; the rightmost single-digit number, the number of the book's printing. For example, a printing code of 94-1 shows that the first printing of the book occurred in 1994.

Screen reproductions in this book were created with Collage Plus from Inner Media, Inc., Hollis, NH.

Publisher: David P. Ewing

Associate Publisher: Michael Miller

Director of Publishing: Don Roche, Jr.

Managing Editor: Michael Cunningham

Product Marketing Manager: Ray Robinson

Credits

Publishing Manager
Charles O. Stewart, III

Acquisitions Editor
Nancy Stevenson

Product Directors
Joyce J. Nielsen
Jim Minatel

Product Development
Elden Nelson

Editors
Michael Cunningham
Noelle Gasco
Heather Northrup

Technical Editors
Tish Nye
Richard F. Brown

Book Designer
Amy Peppler-Adams

Cover Designers
Dan Armstrong
Amy Peppler-Adams

Production Team
Angela Bannan
Claudia Bell
Cameron Booker
Anne Dickerson
Karen Dodson
Teresa Forrester
Joelynn Gifford
Elizabeth Lewis
Andrea Marcum
Linda Quigley
Caroline Roop
Dennis Sheehan
Sue VandeWalle
Tim Montgomery
Amy Steed
Tina Trettin
Mary Beth Wakefield
Donna Winter

Indexer
Jennifer Eberhardt

Composed in *Stone* and *MCPdigital* by Que Corporation

About the Authors

Ron Holmes, computer coordinator for the Metropolitan School District of Wayne Township in Indianapolis, Indiana, assists in the acquisition, installation, and maintenance of all computer-related applications within the school district. He teaches dBASE, PC Operating Systems, and Lotus 1-2-3 for a local college, and also runs a consulting business that provides custom programming database management and preventative maintenance service. Since 1985, Ron has served as a technical editor for Que Corporation and New Riders Publishing, providing technical support on more than 25 books. He is co-author of *Using Norton Desktop for DOS*, *Using Microsoft Works 3 for DOS*, and *Using Norton Utilities 7*. Ron is currently working on his MBA and hopes to complete his course of study very soon.

Elden Nelson, Senior Writer at Que, is the author of *I Hate WordPerfect 6 for Windows* and a number of other WordPerfect books. He is a columnist for both *WordPerfect Magazine* and *WordPerfect for Windows Magazine*. He welcomes your comments on this book. You can reach Elden c/o Que or on CompuServe at 75120,1523.

Trademark Acknowledgments

All terms mentioned in this book that are known to be trademarks or service marks have been appropriately capitalized. Que Corporation cannot attest to the accuracy of this information. Use of a term in this book should not be regarded as affecting the validity of any trademark or service mark.

Contents

How to Use This Book

Welcome to a revolutionary concept in quick references! Unlike traditional pocket references, which usually pack a lot of text on the page but few, if any, illustrations, the *VisiRef* series presents nearly all of its "how-to" information *visually*. You'll find all the essential tasks here, color-coded and organized alphabetically by larger task category. Use the color-coded sections to quickly locate the task you need to find, follow the full-color screen shots to see each step in the process, and then complete the task yourself. If you're someone who prefers to learn or recall information by being *shown* how a task is accomplished, Que's *VisiRef* series is well matched to your needs. The *VisiRef* books are the perfect complement to today's graphical software. You don't have to read a lot of text to find the reference information you need.

Each page provides the following information:

Color-coded pages make it easy to find the task category you need.

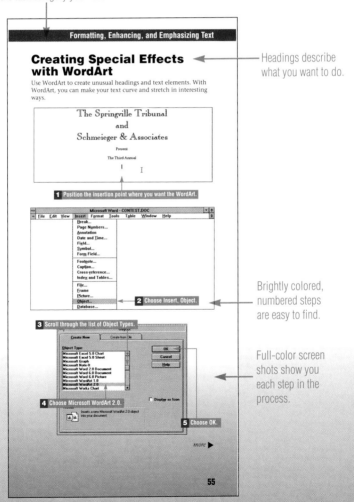

Headings describe what you want to do.

Brightly colored, numbered steps are easy to find.

Full-color screen shots show you each step in the process.

Typing, Moving, and Deleting Text

Whether creating a new document or adding text to an existing document, Word performs text input with relative ease. Word automatically moves text to the next line when necessary, and allows for the easy insertion, replacement, and deletion of text.

To type in Word

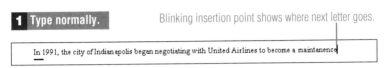

1 Type normally.

Blinking insertion point shows where next letter goes.

In 1991, the city of Indianapolis began negotiating with United Airlines to become a maintanence

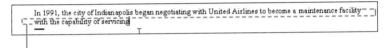

2 Do not press Enter at the end of each line; Just keep typing.

In 1991, the city of Indianapolis began negotiating with United Airlines to become a maintenance facility with the capability of servicing

When text goes past the margin, Word automatically moves it to the next line.

To insert new text in the middle of existing text

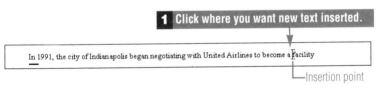

1 Click where you want new text inserted.

In 1991, the city of Indianapolis began negotiating with United Airlines to become a Facility

Insertion point

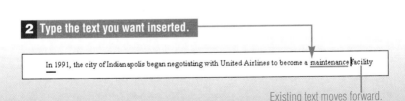

2 Type the text you want inserted.

In 1991, the city of Indianapolis began negotiating with United Airlines to become a maintenance Facility

Existing text moves forward.

3

Paragraph and Page Breaks

Word automatically ends lines, but it is up to you to tell it when to end a paragraph. Word also ends pages automatically when the text you enter exceeds the number of lines allotted per page (usually 66) unless you tell it otherwise.

To end a paragraph

1 The insertion point should be at the end of the last sentence in a paragraph.

In 1991, the city of Indianapolis began negotiating with United Airlines to become a maintenance center. The cost to the City of Indianapolis, the State of Indiana, Hendricks County, and the Indianapolis Airport Authority is in excess of $250 million dollars. The question asked by many Hoosiers has been "Who is going to pay? Is the cost to the citizens of this state justified by the number of jobs created, or the influx of new business to the area?" These are questions that can only be answered as construction draws to a close and maintenance operations begin.

United Airlines also has a stake in the successful implementation of this huge undertaking. Their estimated cost will exceed $500 million, and should the employment projections and average salary fall short, United Airlines will be required to reimburse state and local government agencies a fixed percentage.

2 Press Enter to begin a new paragraph.

To create a blank line between paragraphs, press Enter again.

When it's time for a new page

Word automatically starts a new page when text goes beyond the bottom margin.

created, or the influx of new business to the area?" These are questions that can only be answered as construction draws to a close and maintenance operations begin.

United Airlines also has a stake in the successful implementation of this huge undertaking. Their estimated cost will exceed $500 million, and should the employment projections and average salary fall short, United Airlines will be required to reimburse state and local government agencies a fixed percentage.

The new facitility will be constructed on approximately 300 acres of land located at Indianapolis International Airport. About 3 million square feet (all under roof) will be available for (1) and engine shop, (2) shipping and receiving, (3) airframe supply, (4) a component shop, (5) an auto shop, (6) general facitilites and central site, (7) a computer center, (8) security commons, and (9) support shops and aircraft bays.

Page break indicator

If you want to specify the location of a page break

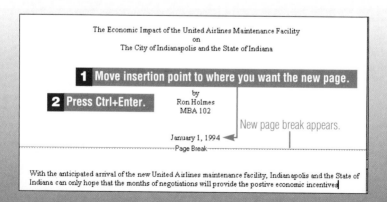

The Economic Impact of the United Airlines Maintenance Facility
on
The City of Indianapolis and the State of Indiana

1 Move insertion point to where you want the new page.

2 Press Ctrl+Enter.

by
Ron Holmes
MBA 102

New page break appears.

January 1, 1994
Page Break

With the anticipated arrival of the new United Airlines maintenance facility, Indianapolis and the State of Indiana can only hope that the months of negotiations will provide the positive economic incentives

Moving the Insertion Point

Your ability to move the insertion point will greatly enhance your ability to edit the documents you create. Moving the insertion point allows you to add, delete, and format text.

To move the insertion point to a place on the screen

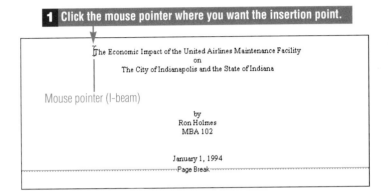

1 Click the mouse pointer where you want the insertion point.

The Economic Impact of the United Airlines Maintenance Facility
on
The City of Indianapolis and the State of Indiana

Mouse pointer (I-beam)

by
Ron Holmes
MBA 102

January 1, 1994
Page Break

To move the insertion point using the keyboard

Key	Action
Up/Down	Move up or down one line
Left/Right	Move left or right one character
Home+Left/End	Move to beginning or end of line
Ctrl+Left/Ctrl+Right	Move left/right one word
Ctrl+Up/Ctrl+Down	Move up/down one paragraph
Crtl+Home/Ctrl+End	Move to beginning or end of document

To use the scroll bar to move

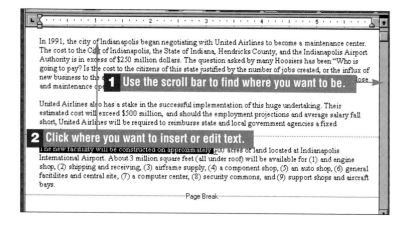

In 1991, the city of Indianapolis began negotiating with United Airlines to become a maintenance center. The cost to the City of Indianapolis, the State of Indiana, Hendricks County, and the Indianapolis Airport Authority is in excess of $250 million dollars. The question asked by many Hoosiers has been "Who is going to pay? Is the cost to the citizens of this state justified by the number of jobs created, or the influx of new business to the s[...] [...]ose and maintenance op[...]

1 Use the scroll bar to find where you want to be.

United Airlines also has a stake in the successful implementation of this huge undertaking. Their estimated cost will exceed $500 million, and should the employment projections and average salary fall short, United Airlines will be required to reimburse state and local government agencies a fixed

2 Click where you want to insert or edit text.

The new facility will be constructed on approximately 500 acres of land located at Indianapolis International Airport. About 3 million square feet (all under roof) will be available for (1) and engine shop, (2) shipping and receiving, (3) airframe supply, (4) a component shop, (5) an auto shop, (6) general facilites and central site, (7) a computer center, (8) security commons, and (9) support shops and aircraft bays.

Page Break

How the scrollbar works

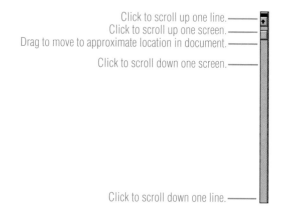

Click to scroll up one line.
Click to scroll up one screen.
Drag to move to approximate location in document.

Click to scroll down one screen.

Click to scroll down one line.

To go to a certain page in a document

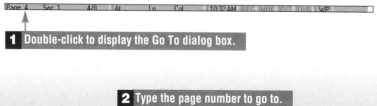

Page 4   Sec 1   4/8   At   Ln   Col   10:32 AM REC MRK EXT OVR WP

1 Double-click to display the Go To dialog box.

2 Type the page number to go to.

3 Click Go To.

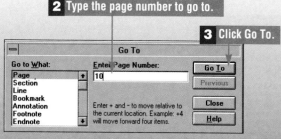

Go To		
Go to What:	Enter Page Number:	Go To
Page	10	Previous
Section		
Line		
Bookmark		
Annotation	Enter + and – to move relative to	Close
Footnote	the current location. Example: +4	
Endnote	will move forward four items.	Help

Selecting Text

Knowing how to select text is a crucial skill to have in Word. When you have selected text, you can change its appearance, move it, or delete it.

To select any amount of text with a mouse

1 Click at the beginning; hold down the mouse button.

The new facility will be constructed on approximately 800 acres of land located at Indianapolis International Airport. About 3 million square feet (all under roof) will be available for (1) and engine shop, (2) shipping and receiving, (3) airframe supply, (4) a component shop, (5) an auto shop, (6) general facitilites and central site, (7) a computer center, (8) security commons, and (9) support shops and aircraft bays.

2 Drag to the end of the selection.

To select a certain amount of text with the mouse

1 Move mouse pointer to where you want selected text.

Click in the selection bar to the left of the line to select that line.

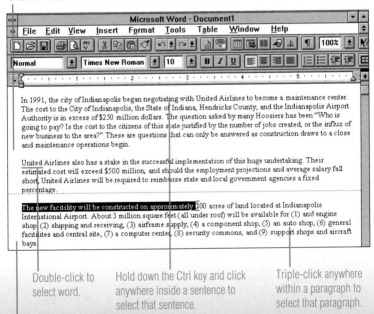

Double-click to select word.

Hold down the Ctrl key and click anywhere inside a sentence to select that sentence.

Triple-click anywhere within a paragraph to select that paragraph.

Triple-click in the selection bar to choose the entire document.

7

To select text from one point to another

1 Click at the beginning of text you want to select.

2 Move mouse pointer to where end of selection should be.

In 1991, the city of Indianapolis began negotiating with United Airlines to become a maintenance center. The cost to the City of Indianapolis, the State of Indiana, Hendricks County, and the Indianapolis Airport Authority is in excess of $250 million dollars. The question asked by many Hoosiers has been "Who is going to pay? Is the cost to the citizens of this state justified by the number of jobs created, or the influx of new business to the area

3 Hold down the Shift key and click the mouse button.

To select text using the keyboard

Key(s)	Action
Shift+Right	Select one character to right
Shift+Left	Select one character to left
Ctrl+Shift+Right	Select to end of a word
Ctrl+Shift+Left	Select to beginning of word
Shift+End	Select to end of line
Shift+Home	Select to beginning of line
Shift+Down	Select down one line
Shift+Up	Select up one line
Ctrl+Shift+Down	Select to end of paragraph
Ctrl+Shift+Up	Select to beginning of paragraph
Shift+Page Up	Select to beginning of page
Shift+Page Down	Select to end of page
Ctrl+Shift+End	Select to end of document
Ctrl+Shift+Home	Select to beginning of document
Ctrl+A	Select entire document

Deleting Text

You can remove unwanted text one character at a time, or in as large of selected blocks as you wish.

Press Backspace to delete the character to the left of the insertion point.

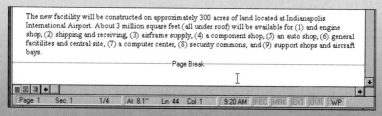

The new facitility will be constructed on approximately 300 acres of land located at Indianapolis International Airport. About 3 million square feet (all under roof) will be available for (1) and engine shop, (2) shipping and receiving, (3) airframe supply, (4) a component shop, (5) an auto shop, (6) general facitilites and central site, (7) a computer center, (8) security commons, and (9) support shops and aircraft bays.

Page Break

| Page 1 | Sec 1 | 1/4 | At 8.1" | Ln 44 | Col 1 | 9:20 AM | REC | MRK | EXT | OVR | WP |

Press Delete to delete character to right of insertion point.

To quickly delete a word using the keyboard

Key(s)	Action
Ctrl+Backspace	Delete one word to the left
Ctrl+Delete	Delete one word to the right

To delete a block of text

1 Select the text you want to delete.

and maintenance operations begin.

United Airlines also has a stake in the successful implementation of this huge undertaking. Their estimated cost will exceed $500 million, and should the employment projections and average salary fall short, United Airlines will be required to reimburse state and local government agencies a fixed percentage.

2 Press Delete.

The new facitility will be constructed on app...   cated at Indianapolis

And maintenance operations begin.

a stake in the successful implementation of this huge undertaking. Their estimated cost will exceed $500 million, and should the employment projections and average salary fall short, United Airlines will be required to reimburse state and local government agancies a fixed percentage.

The new facitility will be constructed on approximately 300 acres of land located at Indianapolis

Text moves to take deleted text's place.

To replace a block of text with new text

1 Select text to be replaced.

percentage.

The new facitility will be constructed on approximately 300 acres of land located at Indianapolis International Airport. About 3 million square feet (all under roof) will be available for (1) and engine shop, (2) shipping and receiving, (3) airframe supply, (4) a component shop, (5) an auto shop, (6) general facitilites and central site, (7) a computer center, (8) security commons, and (9) support shops and aircraft bays.

————Page Break————

2 Type text to replace selected text.

percentage.

The new building will be constructed on approximately 300 acres of land located at Indianapolis International Airport. About 3 million square feet (all under roof) will be available for (1) and engine shop, (2) shipping and receiving, (3) airframe supply, (4) a component shop, (5) an auto shop, (6) general facitilites and central site, (7) a computer center, (8) security commons, and (9) support shops and aircraft

Selected text disappears and is replaced by new text.

Correcting Mistakes

If you accidentally delete text you need back, there is no need to retype it. Use the Undo feature to bring it back. If you make other types of mistakes, such as pressing Enter when you did not mean to, use Undo to reverse your most recent action.

To undo mistakes

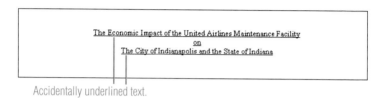

Accidentally underlined text.

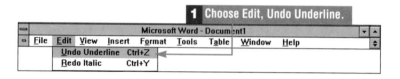

Underlining is removed from selected text.

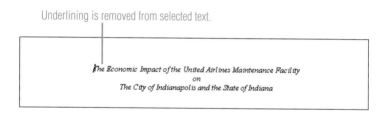

To restore deleted text

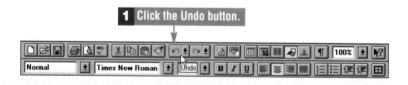

Deleted text reappears.

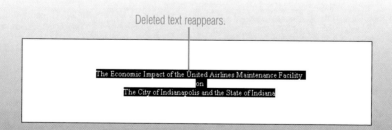

Finding and Replacing Text

In long documents, it may be difficult to locate a certain word or phrase. Word can quickly take you to it. You can also replace a given word or phrase with another.

To find text

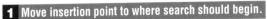
1 Move insertion point to where search should begin.

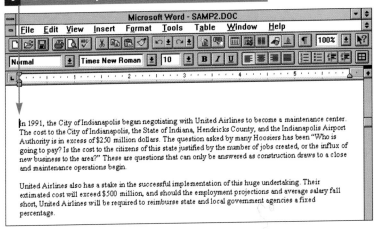

In 1991, the City of Indianapolis began negotiating with United Airlines to become a maintenance center. The cost to the City of Indianapolis, the State of Indiana, Hendricks County, and the Indianapolis Airport Authority is in excess of $250 million dollars. The question asked by many Hoosiers has been "Who is going to pay? Is the cost to the citizens of this state justified by the number of jobs created, or the influx of new business to the area?" These are questions that can only be answered as construction draws to a close and maintenance operations begin.

United Airlines also has a stake in the successful implementation of this huge undertaking. Their extimated cost will exceed $500 million, and should the employment projections and average salary fall short, United Airlines will be required to reimburse state and local government agencies a fixed percentage.

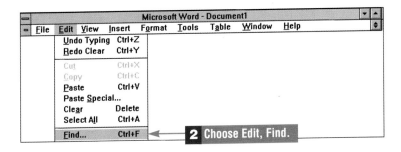
2 Choose Edit, Find.

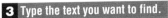
3 Type the text you want to find.

4 Select desired options in dialog box.

5 Choose Find Next.

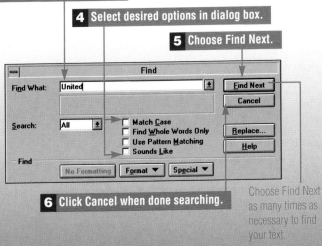

6 Click Cancel when done searching.

Choose Find Next as many times as necessary to find your text.

To replace text

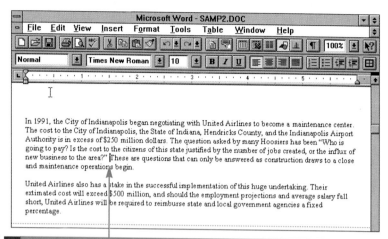

1 Move insertion to point where you want to begin searching for text to replace.

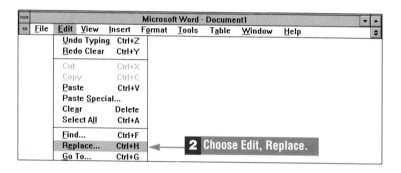

2 Choose Edit, Replace.

3 Type the text to find.

4 Type text to replace it with.

5 Select desired options in dialog box.

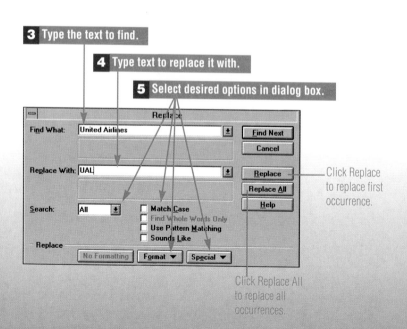

Click Replace to replace first occurrence.

Click Replace All to replace all occurrences.

Inserting the Date

In most documents you create, you may have a need to incorporate the date. Word lets you quickly insert the current date into your document. The date can be updated automatically if you so desire, or you can have the date remain constant.

1 Move insertion point to where you want date to appear.

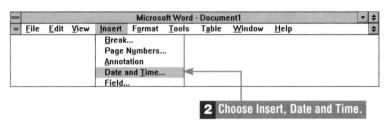

2 Choose Insert, Date and Time.

3 Select desired date format.

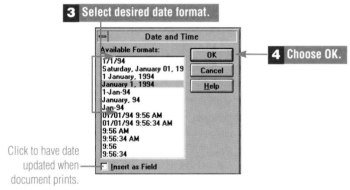

4 Choose OK.

Click to have date updated when document prints.

Using Tabs and Indents

Many writing styles call for the first line of each paragraph to be indented. You may also want to create a hanging indent or indent the entire paragraph.

To insert a tab at the beginning of a paragraph

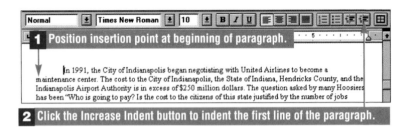

1 Position insertion point at beginning of paragraph.

In 1991, the City of Indianapolis began negotiating with United Airlines to become a maintenance center. The cost to the City of Indianapolis, the State of Indiana, Hendricks County, and the Indianapolis Airport Authority is in excess of $250 million dollars. The question asked by many Hoosiers has been "Who is going to pay? Is the cost to the citizens of this state justified by the number of jobs

2 Click the Increase Indent button to indent the first line of the paragraph.

To indent the entire paragraph

United Airlines also has a stake in the successful implementation of this huge undertaking. Their estimated cost will exceed $500 million, and should the employment projections and average salary fall short, United Airlines will be required to reimburse state and local government agencies a fixed percentage.

1 Position the insertion point in paragraph.

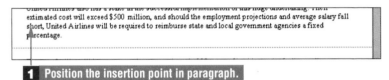

2 Choose Format, Paragraph.

3 Choose the Indents and Spacing tab.

Hanging—Entering a negative number will cause a hanging indent.

First Line—Entering a positive number will cause only the first line of paragraph to be indented.

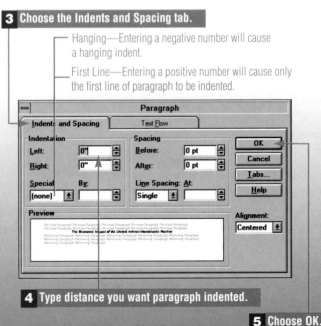

4 Type distance you want paragraph indented.

5 Choose OK.

Working with Section Breaks

Using section breaks, you can identify sections for organization and formatting purposes. Section breaks are created for the purpose of changing different elements in a portion of the document.

Creating Section Breaks

To insert new text in the middle of existing

1 Move insertion point to where you want a new section to begin.

Pros
1. Generates good will in the community. The public perceives the Tribunal as doing something beyond the traditional call of the newspaper. By encouraging youth to write and giving prizes, we show ourselves to be interested in the city.
2. Increases Circulation: The issue in which we announce the contest, as well as the issue in which we announce winners, have been big sellers, drawing people who ordinarily don't purchase a paper.
3. Discovers Talent: The First Place winner from last year's contest now works with our staff during the summers and intends to study Journalism at college.

2 Choose Insert, Break.

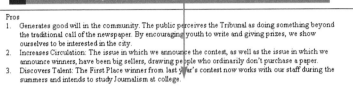

Microsoft Word - CONTEST.DOC

File   Edit   View   Insert   Format   Tools   Table   Window   Help

Break...
Page Numbers...

3 Choose the Section Option appropriate for your needs.

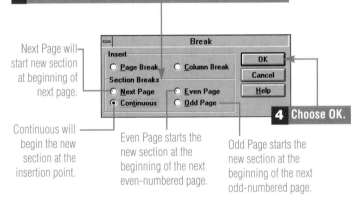

Next Page will start new section at beginning of next page.

Continuous will begin the new section at the insertion point.

Even Page starts the new section at the beginning of the next even-numbered page.

Odd Page starts the new section at the beginning of the next odd-numbered page.

4 Choose OK.

To delete a section break

1 Move insertion point immediately below the section break mark.

Pros
1. Generates good will in the community. The public perceives the Tribunal as doing something beyond the traditional call of the newspaper. By encouraging youth to write and giving prizes, we show ourselves to be interested in the city.
2. Increases Circulation: The issue in which we announce the contest, as well as the issue in which we announce winners, have been big sellers, drawing people who ordinarily don't purchase a paper.
3. Discovers Talent: The First Place winner from last year's contest now works with our staff during the summers and intends to study Journalism at college.
================End of Section================
4.

Cons

2 Press Backspace.

All formatting associated with deleted section break is also deleted.

Viewing a Document in Page Layout Mode

Word's Page Layout mode gives you a close look at how your document will appear when printed. Headers, footers, margins, page numbers, and other formatting all appear on-screen as they will when printed. This is a good general-purpose view mode for writing, editing, and formatting.

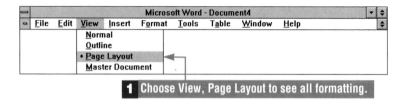

1 Choose View, Page Layout to see all formatting.

Viewing a Document in Normal Mode

In the Normal view mode, Word does not show headers, footers, top and bottom margins, and some other formatting. When you are concentrating on writing and editing text—not formatting—the Normal mode gives you more room to see your text.

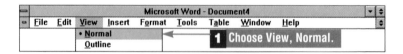

1 Choose View, Normal.

Viewing Multiple Pages of a Document

Use the Zoom mode in conjunction with Page Layout mode when you what to get a general idea of how facing and/or multiple pages will appear. Because of the text size displayed in this mode, this is not a good mode for writing or editing.

1 Be certain that you are in Page Layout mode.

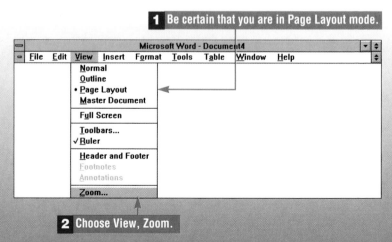

2 Choose View, Zoom.

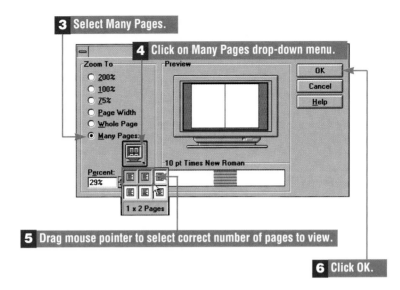

3 Select Many Pages.

4 Click on Many Pages drop-down menu.

Zoom To
○ 200%
○ 100%
○ 75%
○ Page Width
○ Whole Page
◉ Many Pages

Preview

OK
Cancel
Help

Percent:
29%

10 pt Times New Roman

1 x 2 Pages

5 Drag mouse pointer to select correct number of pages to view.

6 Click OK.

Showing Paragraph Marks

Under normal circumstances you cannot see the underlying commands that make the "white space" of a document—ends of paragraphs, tabs, spaces, and so on. You can make these symbols visible, letting you know where they have been put.

1 Click Show/Hide ¶.

Normal   Times New Roman   2   B I U   Show/Hide ¶

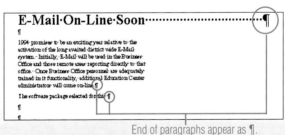

E-Mail·On-Line·Soon·······················¶

1994 promises to be an exciting year relative to the activation of the long awaited district wide E-Mail system. Initially, E-Mail will be used in the Business Office and those remote users reporting directly to that office. Once Business Office personnel are adequately trained in it functionality, additional Education Center administrators will come on-line.¶

The software package selected for this¶

End of paragraphs appear as ¶.

Maximizing Editing Space

You can turn off all of Word's on-screen tools for more writing and editing space.

Screen tools limit your workspace.   Title bar   Menu bar   Rulers   Toolbars

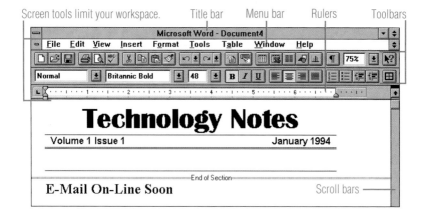

Scroll bars ——

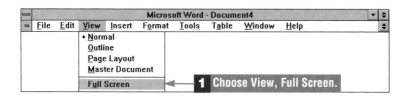

1 Choose View, Full Screen.

More space for writing and editing.

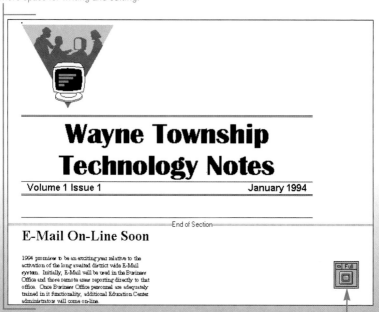

2 To bring toolbars and rulers back, click the Full Screen icon.

18

Changing the Size of On-Screen Text

The Zoom feature functions in much the same fashion as a microscope—it lets you magnify the text on-screen up to 200%. You can also make the text appear smaller, to see more of the page at once. The Zoom feature does not affect how large the text will be when it prints.

1 Click the Zoom drop-down menu.

2 Click desired option.

Show close-up view.

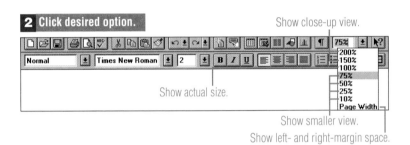

Show actual size.

Show smaller view.

Show left- and right-margin space.

Technology Notes

Volume 1 Issue 1	January 1994

End of Section

E-Mail On-Line Soon

1994 promises to be an exciting year relative to the activation of the long awaited district wide E-Mail system. Initially, E-Mail will be used in the Business Office. Once Business Office personnel are adequately trained in its functionality, additional Education Center administrators will come on-line.

Thereafter we anticipate a roll-out for this

Text zoomed to 50%.

E-Mail On-Line Soon

1994 promises to be an exciting year relative to the activation of the long awaited district wide E-Mail system. Initially, E-Mail will be used in the Business Office and those remote areas reporting directly to that

Text zoomed to 200%

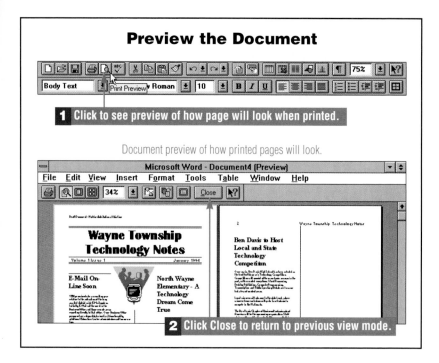

Preview the Document

1 Click to see preview of how page will look when printed.

Document preview of how printed pages will look.

2 Click Close to return to previous view mode.

Looking at Paragraph Formatting

Word does not use formatting codes to illustrate formatting. All formatting is shown on-screen the way it will be printed. However, you can check to see what formatting is applied to a particular section of text.

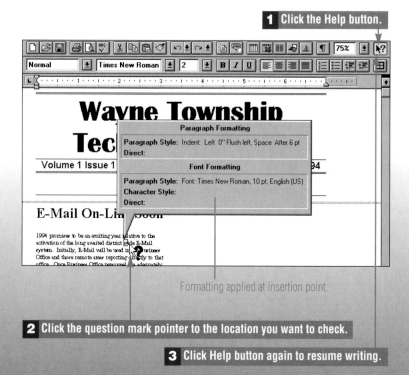

1 Click the Help button.

Formatting applied at insertion point.

2 Click the question mark pointer to the location you want to check.

3 Click Help button again to resume writing.

Splitting the Window

There may be times when you wish to work with more than one part of a document. Word's ability to split a document into two panes allows for editing two portions of your document without scrolling back and forth.

Splitting the window into panes

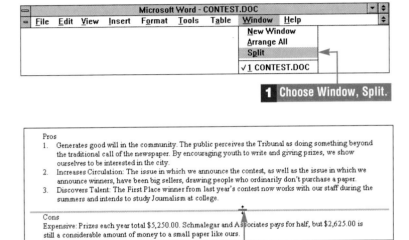

1 Choose Window, Split.

2 Drag the scroll drag to where you want your window split.

3 Click the left mouse button.

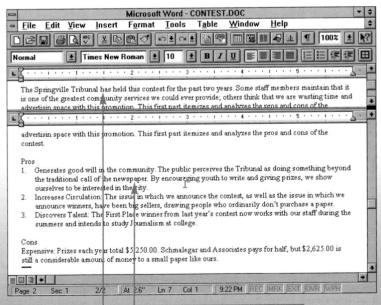

4 Click in a pane and use the scroll bars to move normally.

Changes made in one pane will be reflected in the other.

To delete the split

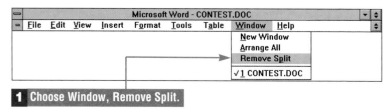

1 Choose Window, Remove Split.

Working with Outlines

Outlining offers a structure upon which you can build your ideas, then fill in the details. Collapsing and expanding elements of an outline allow for quick navigation throughout the outlined document.

To create an outline

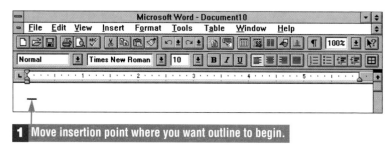

1 Move insertion point where you want outline to begin.

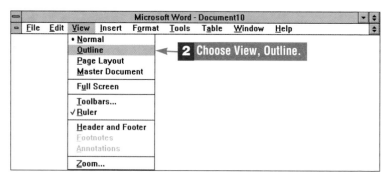

2 Choose View, Outline.

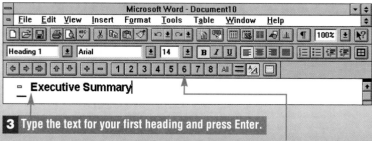

3 Type the text for your first heading and press Enter.

The Outline bar appears at top of document.

4 Type additional outline entries.

To demote a heading

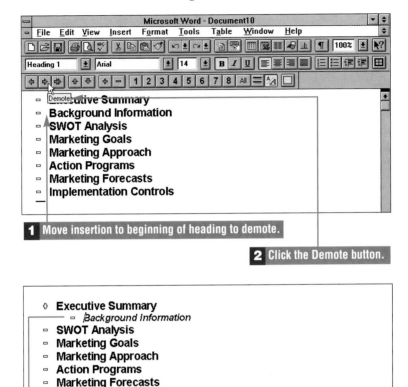

1 Move insertion to beginning of heading to demote.

2 Click the Demote button.

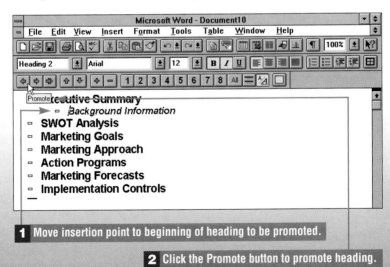

Heading demoted to a level 2 heading.

To promote a heading

1 Move insertion point to beginning of heading to be promoted.

2 Click the Promote button to promote heading.

To move a heading

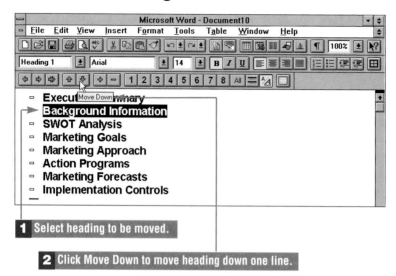

1 Select heading to be moved.

2 Click Move Down to move heading down one line.

Heading will be moved up or down one level for each click of Move Up or Move Down.

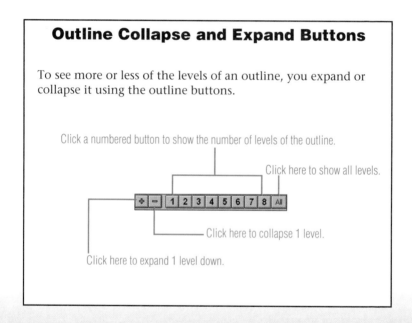

Outline Collapse and Expand Buttons

To see more or less of the levels of an outline, you expand or collapse it using the outline buttons.

Click a numbered button to show the number of levels of the outline.

Click here to show all levels.

Click here to collapse 1 level.

Click here to expand 1 level down.

Working with Master Documents

Word's Master Document feature lets you examine the contents of many small documents, that when combined form a large document or book. Looking much like an outline, a master document draws its material from several subdocuments.

To create a new master document

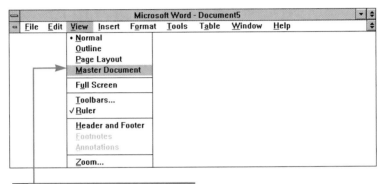

	Microsoft Word - Document5	
File	Edit	View	Insert	Format	Tools	Table	Window	Help

- Normal
  Outline
  Page Layout
  Master Document

  Full Screen

  Toolbars...
  √ Ruler

  Header and Footer
  Footnotes
  Annotations

  Zoom...

1 Choose View, Master Document.

The Master Document toolbar.

⇦ ⇨ ⇧ ⇩ ➕ ➖ 1 2 3 4 5 6 7 8 All ☰ 🅰 ▢ 🗏 🗏 🗏 🗏 🗏 🗏

- Section I: Executive Summary
- Section II: Background Information
- Section III: SWOT Analysis
- Section IV: Marketing Goals
- Section V: Marketing Approach
- Section VI: Action Programs
- Section VII: Marketing Forecasts
- Section VIII: Implementation Controls

2 Begin entering the outline for your document.

Use Word's outline tools and heading styles to suit your needs.

To create a subdocument

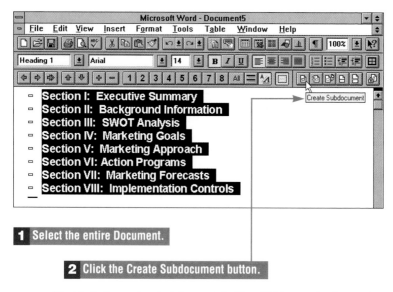

1 Select the entire Document.

2 Click the Create Subdocument button.

Word limits the number of subdocuments to 80 and 32M per master document.

Subdocuments, as they exist in the master document.

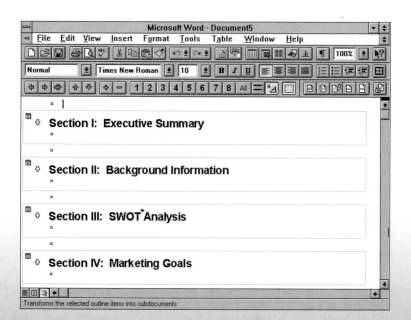

Working with Subdocuments

Subdocuments can be edited in a number of ways. One way would be to perform the edits in the master documents. Second, double-click the document icon, in which case, a new file is opened containing the subdocument. Finally, after saving and closing the master document, you can open the subdocument just as you would any other document.

To edit a subdocument

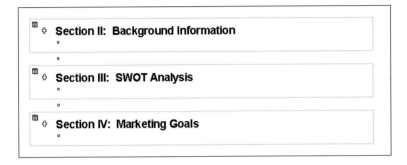

1 Double-click the document icon in the subdocument you want to edit.

A new document window will open.

To return to the master document from a subdocument

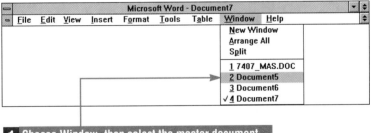

1 Choose Window, then select the master document.

27

Begin a Drawing

To add emphasis and visual impact to your documents, Word lets you draw pictures that can be placed almost anywhere in your document.

1 Move insertion point to where you want drawing inserted.

2 Click the Drawing button.

When you've completed the drawing, you can move it to a different location.

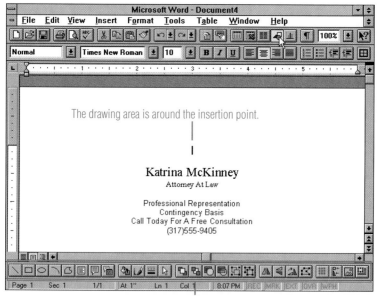

The drawing tools

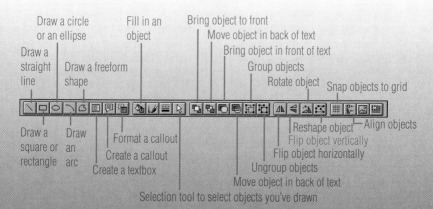

Draw a circle or an ellipse

Fill in an object

Bring object to front

Move object in back of text

Bring object in front of text

Group objects

Rotate object

Snap objects to grid

Draw a straight line

Draw a freeform shape

Draw a square or rectangle

Draw an arc

Format a callout

Create a callout

Create a textbox

Reshape object

Align objects

Flip object vertically

Flip object horizontally

Ungroup objects

Move object in back of text

Selection tool to select objects you've drawn

Drawing Objects

Most things you draw in Word are created in similar fashion: select the type of object you want to draw from the palette, then click with the mouse to make the object the size most appropriate for your document.

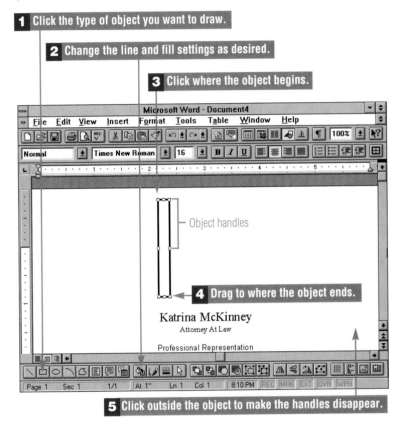

1 Click the type of object you want to draw.

2 Change the line and fill settings as desired.

3 Click where the object begins.

Object handles

4 Drag to where the object ends.

Katrina McKinney
Attorney At Law

Professional Representation

5 Click outside the object to make the handles disappear.

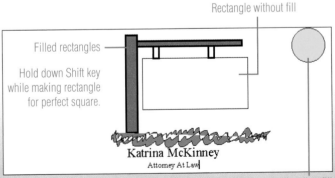

Rectangle without fill

Filled rectangles

Hold down Shift key while making rectangle for perfect square.

Katrina McKinney
Attorney At Law

Oval object with yellow fill

To make a perfect circle, hold down Shift key while making (on drawing) oval.

Adding Text to a Drawing

You can make text a part of your drawing, then size and place it like any other part of the drawing.

1 Click the Text tool.

2 Click the upper-left corner of the area where you want text.

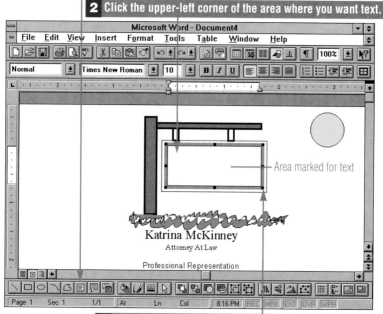

Area marked for text

Katrina McKinney
Attorney At Law

Professional Representation

3 Drag to lower-right corner of where you want text.

4 Choose Format, Font.

5 Select the font you want to use.

6 Select the size you want to use.

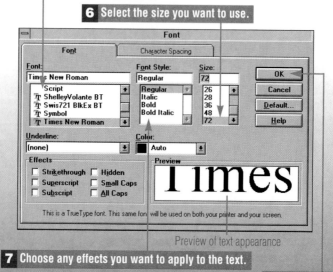

Preview of text appearance

7 Choose any effects you want to apply to the text.

8 Choose OK.

9 Type text you want inserted in textbox.

10 Click outside of text area to make object handles disappear.

Moving and Sizing Objects

Once an object has been created—such as a rectangle, circle, or text—you may find the need to edit it or move it to a different location in your document. You can select the object, then make the necessary changes.

To move an object

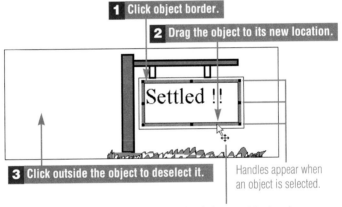

1 Click object border.

2 Drag the object to its new location.

3 Click outside the object to deselect it.

Handles appear when an object is selected.

Cursor is four-headed arrow while dragging.

Object in new location

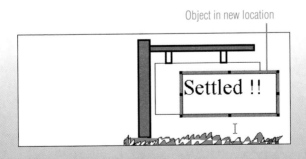

To change the size of an object

1 Click the object to select it.

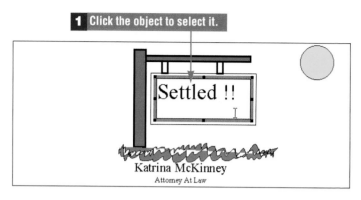

2 Click a handle and drag it in the direction you want to size the object.

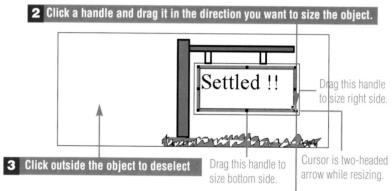

Drag this handle to size right side.

Drag this handle to size bottom side.

Cursor is two-headed arrow while resizing.

3 Click outside the object to deselect

Drag this handle to size right and bottom side.

Editing and Deleting Objects

You can change the color, border, and fill of objects you have created. If you need to, you can delete an object altogether.

To edit an object

1 Click the object to be edited.

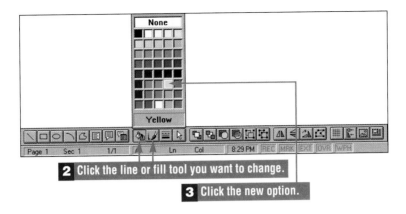

2 Click the line or fill tool you want to change.

3 Click the new option.

4 Click outside the object to deselect it.

Selected object changes.

To delete an object

1 Click the object to be deleted.

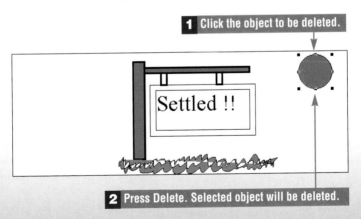

2 Press Delete. Selected object will be deleted.

Returning from Drawing to Word

When your drawing is complete, simply continue editing or adding text. This task can either be continued in Page Layout mode or you can change to Normal mode, in which the picture you just created no longer appears as a part of the document—although it is still there.

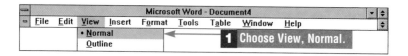

Returning to Drawing from a Word Document

Once you have created your picture and returned to an editing mode, you may find it necessary or desirable to make some changes to the picture. After returning to the draw mode, you can add, edit, and move objects just as you did when you were creating it.

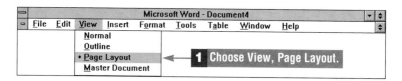

2 Select object to be edited.

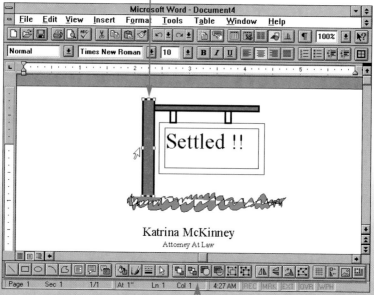

3 Make necessary size, color, or line changes as desired.

Copy and Paste

Use Copy to place a copy of selected text into the computer's memory (Clipboard), while leaving the original text undisturbed. You can then use Paste to insert that text elsewhere in the document, giving you an identical copy of the text in more than one place.

1 Select the text you want to use more than once.

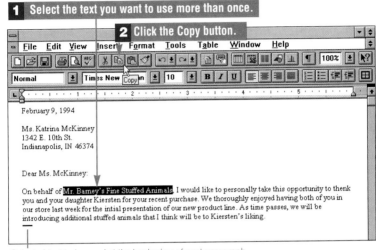

2 Click the Copy button.

Selected text to be used at the beginning of next paragraph.

3 Place the insertion point where you want a copy of the text.

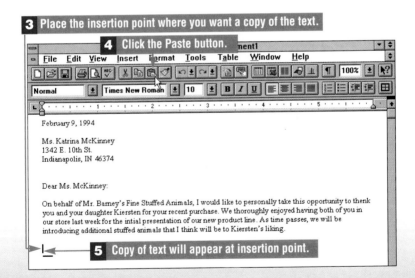

4 Click the Paste button.

5 Copy of text will appear at insertion point.

Cut and Paste

Use the Cut feature to literally remove selected text from a certain place in your document and maintain that text in memory (Clipboard) until you need it again. Use Paste to insert the cut text into a new place in your document.

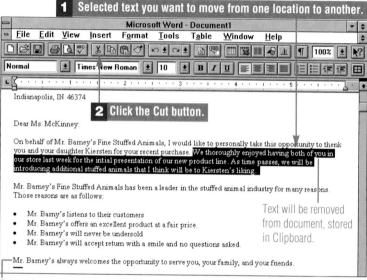

1 Selected text you want to move from one location to another.

2 Click the Cut button.

Text will be removed from document, stored in Clipboard.

Selected text should be after bullet list.

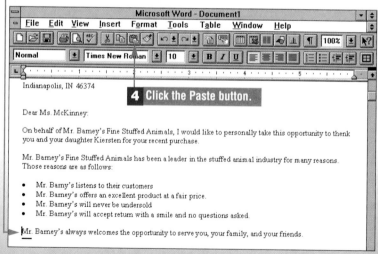

3 Place insertion point where you want the text moved to.

4 Click the Paste button.

Text from Clipboard will be pasted into document.

Drag and Drop

Use the Drag and Drop feature to select text, then quickly move it to a different location in your document. You can also use Drag and Drop to insert a copy of selected text into another place in the document.

To move text using Drag and Drop

1 Select the text you want to move.

RE: Recent Purchase

February 9, 1994

Ms. Katrina McKinney
1342 E. 10th St.
Indianapolis, IN 46374

Selected text needs to be moved here.

Dear Ms. McKinney:

On behalf of Mr. Barney's Fine Stuffed Animals, I would like to personally take this opportunity to thank you and your daughter Kiersten for your recent purchase.

2 Click and hold inside the selected text.

RE: Recent Purchase
February 9, 1994

Ms. Katrina McKinney
1342 E. 10th St.
Indianapolis, IN 46374

Dear Ms. McKinney:

Mouse pointer changes to show text can be dragged and dropped.

RE: Recent Purchase

February 9, 1994

Ms. Katrina McKinney
1342 E. 10th St.
Indianapolis, IN 46374

Insertion point shows where text will begin.
Dear Ms. McKinney:

On behalf of Mr. Barney's Fine Stuffed Animals, I would like to personally take this opportunity to thank you and your daughter Kiersten for your recent purchase.

3 Drag mouse pointer to where you want text moved to.

Selected text is moved to new location.

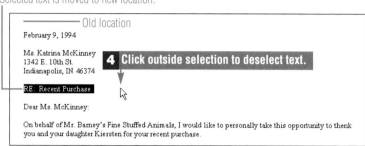

To copy text using Drag and Drop

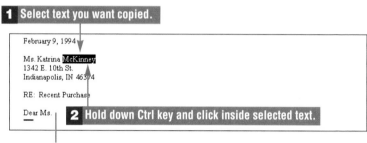

Copy of last name should go here.

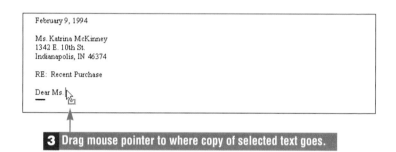

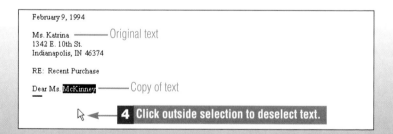

Finding Your Place with Bookmarks

The Bookmark feature lets you jump to a certain place in your document. You can move several bookmarks in a document, each with a descriptive name, making it possible to quickly move from one place to another in your document without complicated searching.

To place a bookmark

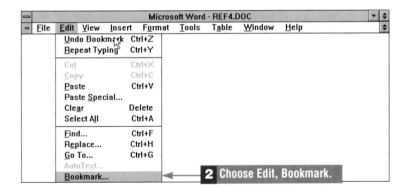

RE: Recent Purchase

Dear Ms. McKinney:

On behalf of Mr. Barney's Fine Stuffed Animals, I would like to personally take this opportunity to thank you and your daughter Kiersten for your recent purchase.

Mr. Barney's Fine Stuffed Animals has been a leader in the stuffed animal industry for many reasons. Those reasons are as follows:

1 Move insertion point to where the bookmark should go.

- Mr. Barney's will never be undersold
- Mr. Barney's will accept return with a smile and no questions asked.

We thoroughly enjoyed having both of you in our store last week for the intial presentation of our new product line. As time passes, we will be introducing additional stuffed animals that I think will be to Kiersten's liking. Mr. Barney's always welcomes the opportunity to serve you, your family, and your friends.

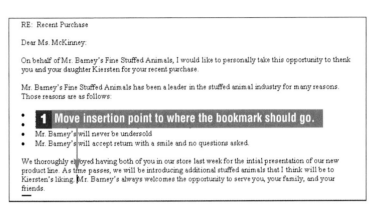

Microsoft Word - REF4.DOC

File | Edit | View | Insert | Format | Tools | Table | Window | Help

Undo Bookmark   Ctrl+Z
Repeat Typing   Ctrl+Y

Cut   Ctrl+X
Copy   Ctrl+C
Paste   Ctrl+V
Paste Special...
Clear   Delete
Select All   Ctrl+A

Find...   Ctrl+F
Replace...   Ctrl+H
Go To...   Ctrl+G
AutoText...
Bookmark...   ◄── **2 Choose Edit, Bookmark.**

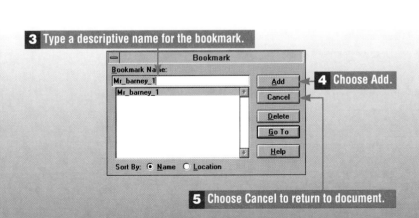

3 Type a descriptive name for the bookmark.

Bookmark

Bookmark Name:
Mr_barney_1   Add   **4 Choose Add.**
Mr_barney_1   Cancel
                            Delete
                            Go To
                            Help

Sort By: ● Name ○ Location

5 Choose Cancel to return to document.

To move to a bookmark within the document

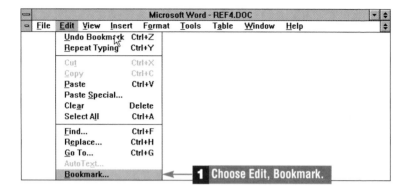

1 Choose Edit, Bookmark.

2 Select the bookmark you want to go to.

3 Click Go To.

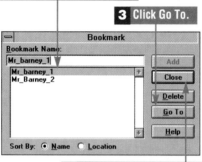

4 Click Close to return to writing or editing.

Insertion point jumps to the bookmark location.

RE: Recent Purchase

Dear Ms. McKinney:

On behalf of Mr. Barney's Fine Stuffed Animals, I would like to personally take this opportunity to thank you and your daughter Kiersten for your recent purchase.

Mr. Barney's Fine Stuffed Animals has been a leader in the stuffed animal industry for many reasons. Those reasons are as follows:

- Mr. Barny's listens to their customers
- Mr. Barney's offers an excellent product at a fair price.
- Mr. Barney's will never be undersold
- Mr. Barney's will accept return with a smile and no questions asked.

We thoroughly enjoyed having both of you in our store last week for the intial presentation of our new product line. As time passes, we will be introducing additional stuffed animals that I think will be to Kiersten's liking. Mr. Barney's always welcomes the opportunity to serve you, your family, and your friends.

Starting a New Document: Saving, Opening, and Working with Files

Starting a new document is like putting a fresh piece of paper in a typewriter. Word lets you work with several documents at once. Your only limitation is the amount of available memory.

1 Click the New document button.

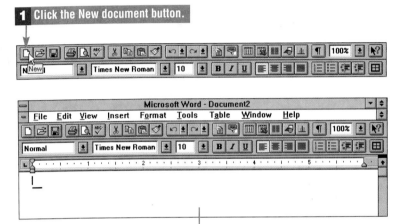

A blank document window appears.

Using Templates

Many documents people create in Word—letters, memos, invoices—are very similar. With the Template feature, you choose a document template that best suits your needs, and Word takes care of the formatting, letting you concentrate on the content of your document.

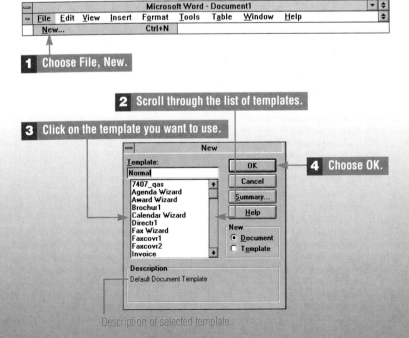

1 Choose File, New.

2 Scroll through the list of templates.

3 Click on the template you want to use.

4 Choose OK.

Description of selected template

43

Using a Word Wizard

Word Wizards step you through the creation of documents with complex or unusual formatting such as calendars, award certificates, and agendas.

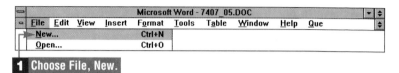

1 Choose File, New.

2 Choose the Wizard you want to use.

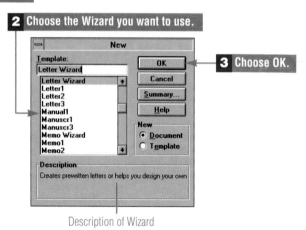

3 Choose OK.

Description of Wizard

4 If a dialog box appears, follow the directions on screen.

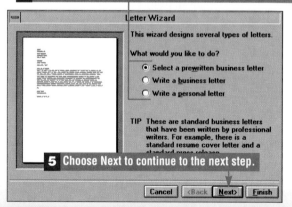

5 Choose Next to continue to the next step.

6 Follow all of the directions and type any needed text.

7 Enter text and edit the document as you normally would in Word.

Saving a Document

You can store a copy of your work on a disk, making it possible to open and edit your work at a later time. Saving a document consists of naming the document, then updating it regularly.

To name a document

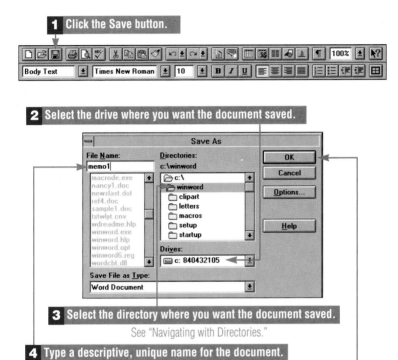

1 Click the Save button.

2 Select the drive where you want the document saved.

3 Select the directory where you want the document saved.

See "Navigating with Directories."

4 Type a descriptive, unique name for the document.

5 Choose OK.

To update the document you're working on

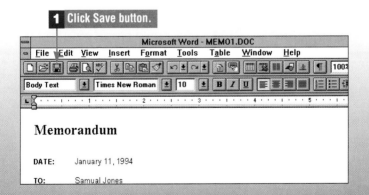

1 Click Save button.

Password-Protecting a Document

If you assign a password, nobody can open the document without knowing the password. The following happens when you click the Options button in the Save As dialog box as shown on the previous page, then continue saving:

1 Follow steps 1-4 in "To name a document." Choose Options.

2 Type a password for the document.

3 Choose OK.

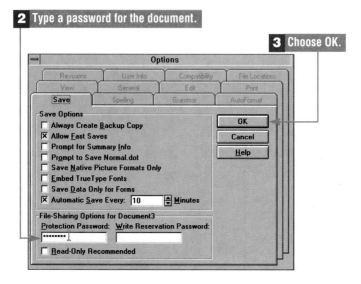

4 Retype password for verification.

5 Choose OK.

Automatically Making Backups

You can have Word save a copy of your document(s) at certain time intervals. By doing so, if a problem—such as a power outage or a computer problem—happens, you are less likely to lose your work.

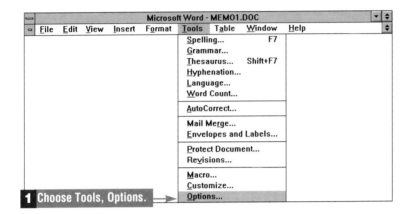

1 Choose Tools, Options.

2 Click the Save tab.

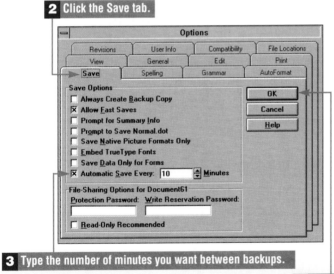

3 Type the number of minutes you want between backups.

4 Choose OK.

47

Closing a Document

Once you have completed your work on a document, you close it. If you have made changes to the document since the last time you saved it, Word offers you the opportunity to save it.

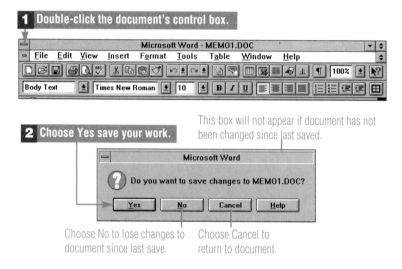

1 Double-click the document's control box.

2 Choose Yes save your work.

This box will not appear if document has not been changed since last saved.

Choose No to lose changes to document since last save.

Choose Cancel to return to document.

Open a Document

Opening a document retrieves a document stored on disk into a document window. When you need to work on a document you've saved and closed, you use the Open feature.

To open a document

1 Click the Open button.

2 Change to the directory containing the file you want.

See "Navigating with Directories."

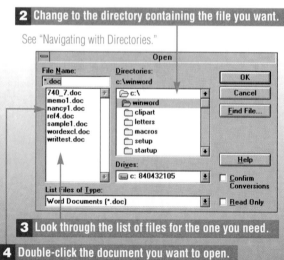

3 Look through the list of files for the one you need.

4 Double-click the document you want to open.

To open a recently used document

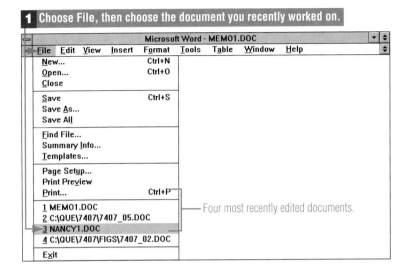

1 Choose File, then choose the document you recently worked on.

Four most recently edited documents.

Navigating with Directories

Use the Open, Save, and other dialog boxes to move from one DOS directory to another, and see what files are in these directories.

1 Choose the Open button.

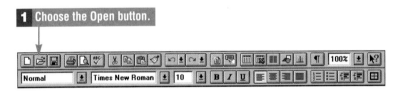

2 Double-click the directory you want to see.

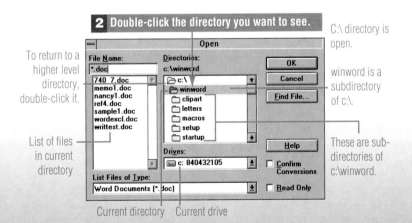

C:\ directory is open.

To return to a higher level directory, double-click it.

winword is a subdirectory of c:\.

List of files in current directory

These are sub-directories of c:\winword.

Current directory   Current drive

Searching for Documents

A document can be located based on any information you can recall about it. You can search any directory and its subdirectories for a file.

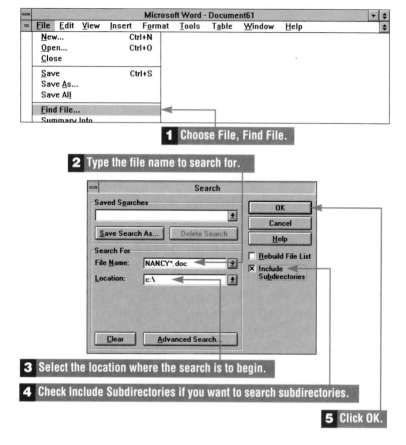

1 Choose File, Find File.

2 Type the file name to search for.

3 Select the location where the search is to begin.

4 Check Include Subdirectories if you want to search subdirectories.

5 Click OK.

Files matching the search criteria   Preview of a file matching the search criteria

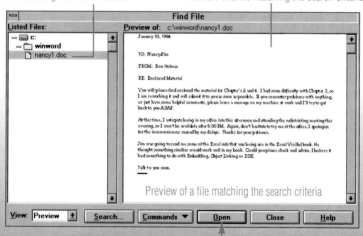

Preview of a file matching the search criteria

6 Click Open to open a file once you find the one you want.

Getting Document Statistics

You can find out the number of words, lines, paragraphs and more in your document with the Document Statistics feature.

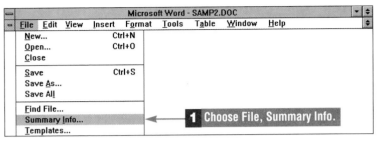

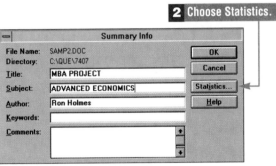

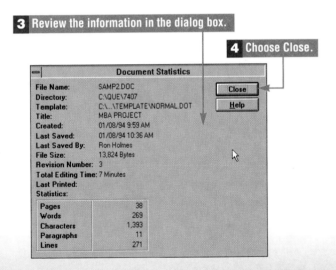

Setting Fonts

A font is the way the letters look on the page. Some fonts are designed to be used as body text in letters and reports, some are designed to be used as decorative headings. Use different fonts in documents to reflect the message of the text.

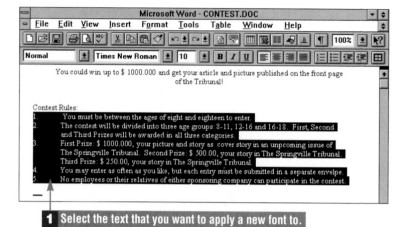

1 Select the text that you want to apply a new font to.

To type new text in a new font, position the insertion point where you want the new font to begin.

2 Choose Format, Font.

3 Click the font you want to use.

4 Click the size you want to use.

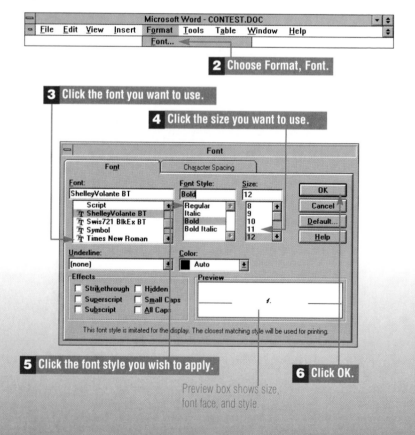

5 Click the font style you wish to apply.

6 Click OK.

Preview box shows size, font face, and style.

Setting a Font Using the Toolbar

If you don't need to see a preview of how the font will look before you select it, you can use Word's Toolbar to quickly set a font and size.

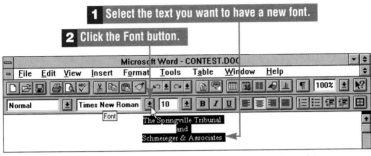

Or place the insertion point where you want the new font to begin applying.

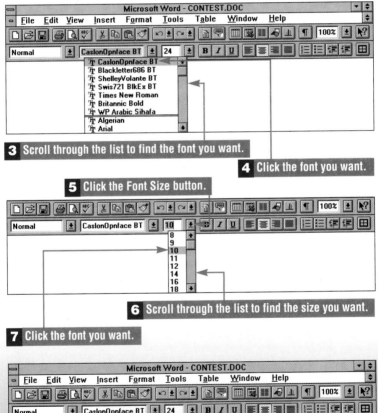

Selected text in new font and size

Setting a Default Font

You probably will use one font more than others, to achieve a consistent look in your documents. You can set this font to the default, so it will automatically be selected when you start a new document.

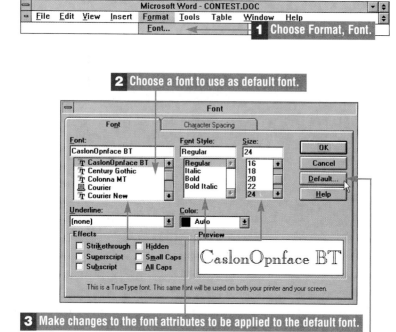

1 Choose Format, Font.

2 Choose a font to use as default font.

3 Make changes to the font attributes to be applied to the default font.

4 Click Default.

5 Click Yes to change the default font.

Microsoft Word

Do you want to change the default font to CaslonOpnface BT, 24 pt?

This change will affect all new documents based on the NORMAL template.

Yes   No   Help

Creating Special Effects with WordArt

Use WordArt to create unusual headings and text elements. With WordArt, you can make your text curve and stretch in interesting ways.

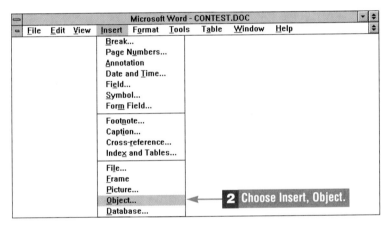

1 Position the insertion point where you want the WordArt.

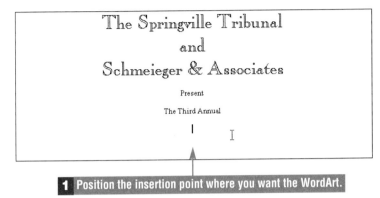

2 Choose Insert, Object.

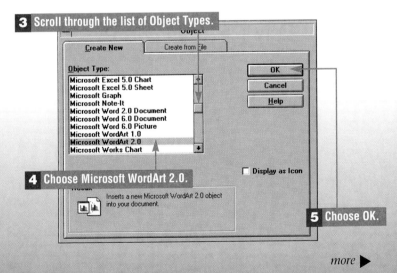

3 Scroll through the list of Object Types.

4 Choose Microsoft WordArt 2.0.

5 Choose OK.

more ▶

Preview window shows how art will look.

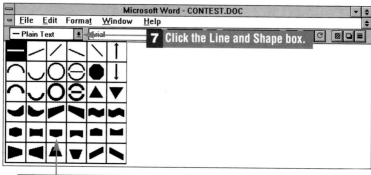

6 Type the text to use with WordArt.

7 Click the Line and Shape box.

8 Click the shape you want the text inserted inside.

Preview of WordArt with text enclosed in shape

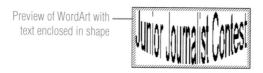

9 Click the Font box to display available fonts to apply to your WordArt.

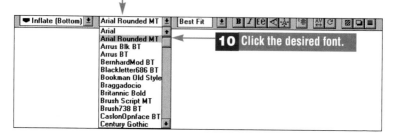

10 Click the desired font.

11 Click outside the WordArt text box to leave WordArt.

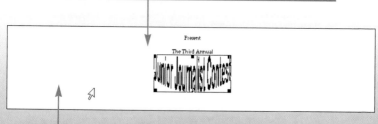

12 Click outside the selected text to deselect it.

Emphasizing and Enhancing Text

Bold, italic, and underline are commonly used to give text emphasis. Word also lets you add emphasis with other font attributes, such as shadowed text, small caps, and outline.

To make selected text bold, underline, or italic

1 Select text to be emphasized.

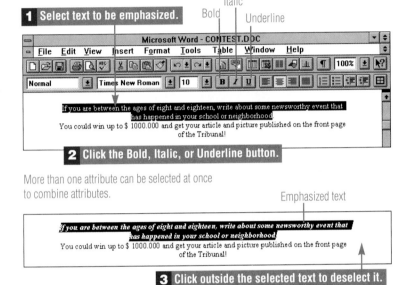

2 Click the Bold, Italic, or Underline button.

More than one attribute can be selected at once to combine attributes.

Emphasized text

3 Click outside the selected text to deselect it.

To make new text bold, italic, or underline

1 Place the insertion point where you want to type.

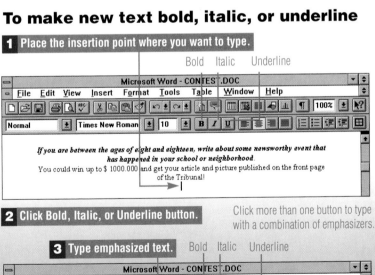

2 Click Bold, Italic, or Underline button.

Click more than one button to type with a combination of emphasizers.

3 Type emphasized text.

4 Click button(s) again to turn off emphasizer(s).

To emphasize text with the menu

1 Select the text you want changed.   Or move to where you want to type.

2 Choose Format, Font.

3 Click the text boxes for the attributes you want to use.

4 Choose OK.

Selected text with new attributes   If you're creating new text, type now.

5 Click outside selection to deselect text.

To turn off attributes

1 Choose Format, Font.

2 Click the text boxes to deselect checked attributes.

3 Choose OK.

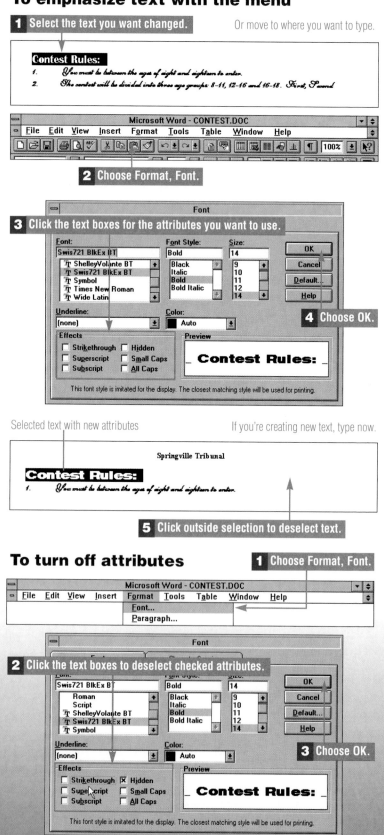

Enhancing Documents Using Drop Caps

Word's Drop Caps feature allows you to draw special attention to portions of your document by enlarging a single character, and then dropping it alongside the first several lines of text.

Part I: Why Have a Junior Journalist Contest?

The Springville Tribunal has held this contest for the past two years. Some staff members maintain that it is one of the greatest community services we could ever provide; others think that we are wasting time and advertisin space with this promotion. This first part itemizes and analyzes the pros and cons of the contest.

1 Select the character where you what a Drop Caps character to appear.

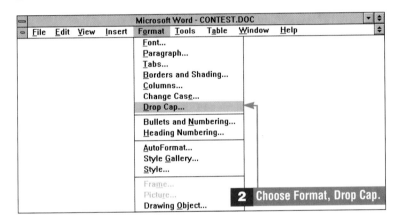

Microsoft Word - CONTEST.DOC

File Edit View Insert Format Tools Table Window Help

Font...
Paragraph...
Tabs...
Borders and Shading...
Columns...
Change Case...
Drop Cap...

Bullets and Numbering...
Heading Numbering...

AutoFormat...
Style Gallery...
Style...

Frame...
Picture...
Drawing Object...

2 Choose Format, Drop Cap.

---

3 Choose one of the three drop caps options.

None. No drop cap.   Dropped. Inserts a drop cap at the selection location.

Drop Cap

Position

None   Dropped   In Margin

Font:
Times New Roman

Lines to Drop: 3

Distance from Text: 0"

OK
Cancel
Help

4 Choose OK.

5 In Margin: Shows as a hanging indent, placing the drop cap in the margin.

Part I: Why Have a Junior Journalist Contest?

The Springville Tribunal has held this contest for the past two years. Some staff members maintain that it is one of the greatest community services we could ever provide; others think that we are wasting time and advertisin space with this promotion. This first part itemizes and analyzes the pros and cons of the contest.

6 Click outside drop cap box to deselect it.

Applying Formatting in More Than One Place

Use styles to consistently apply formatting to text elements such as headings and paragraphs.

1 Select the text containing the format you want.

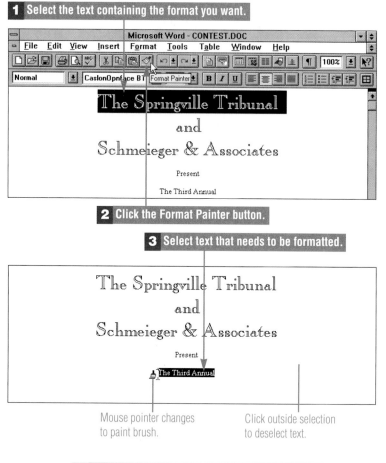

2 Click the Format Painter button.

3 Select text that needs to be formatted.

Mouse pointer changes to paint brush.

Click outside selection to deselect text.

4 Select any other text that needs to be formatted.

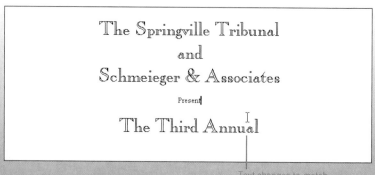

Text changes to match formatted text.

Using Styles for Headings

Use styles to consistently apply formatting to text elements such as headings and paragraphs.

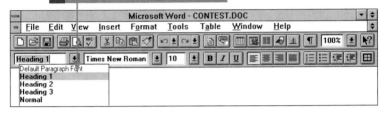

Use lowest-numbered styles for most important heading.

Part I: Why Have a Junior Journalist Contest?

The Springville Tribunal has held this contest for the past two years. Some staff members maintain that it is one of the greatest community services we could ever provide; others think that we are wasting time and advertisin space with this promotion. This first part itemizes and analyzes the pros and cons of the

Formatted heading

To number lists

Use the Numbering button to add numbers to lists. These numbers will be updated automatically when you add or delete list items.

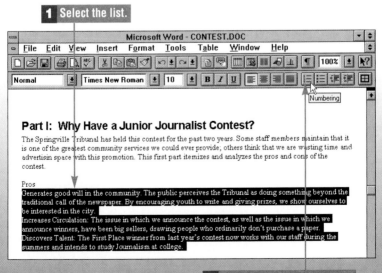

Setting Tabs

Use tabs to line up columns of text or numbers. The Ruler gives you a graphical bar to quickly place and change tabs.

To turn the Ruler bar on or off

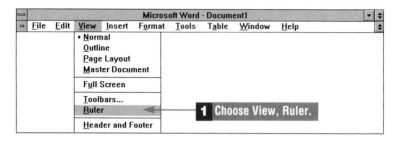

1 Choose View, Ruler.

Tab stops

To add a tab stop

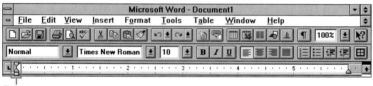

1 Select area where you want tab stop to apply.

2 Click the Tab Alignment button until the desired tab type is showing.

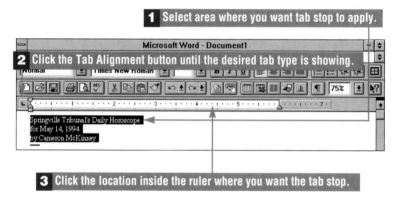

Springville Tribunal's Daily Horoscope
for May 14, 1994
by Cameron McKinney

3 Click the location inside the ruler where you want the tab stop.

To remove one tab stop

1 Depress and hold down the mouse key on tab you don't need .

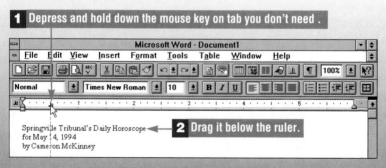

Springville Tribunal's Daily Horoscope
for May 14, 1994
by Cameron McKinney

2 Drag it below the ruler.

To remove all tab stops

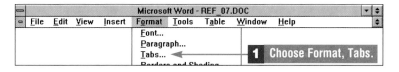

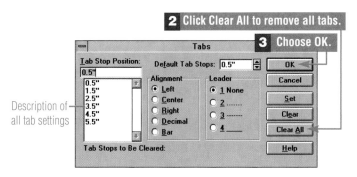

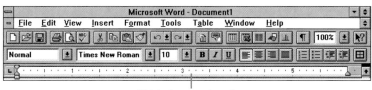

All tab stops are cleared.

Setting Specialized Tab Stops

Besides regular tabs, you can set centered and right-aligned tabs in Word. You can also have a variety of leaders lead up to your tabbed text.

To set left, right, center, and decimal tabs

Examples of Tab Types

Decimal tab stop

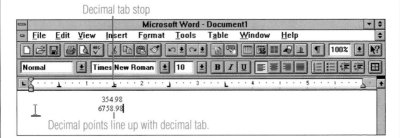

Decimal points line up with decimal tab.

Text is centered around tab.

Center tab stop

Right tab stop

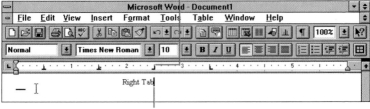

Right edge of text aligns with tab.

Left edge of text aligns with tab stop.

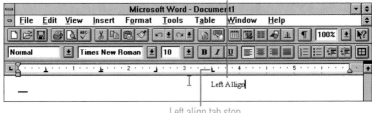

Left align tab stop.

To set tab stops with dot, dash, or line leaders

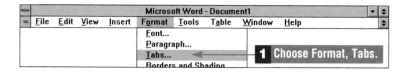

1 Choose Format, Tabs.

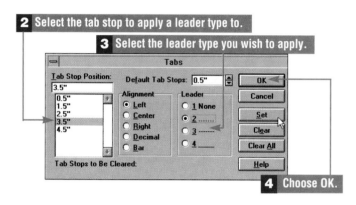

2 Select the tab stop to apply a leader type to.

3 Select the leader type you wish to apply.

4 Choose OK.

Dot leader —— Left tab stop with dot leader

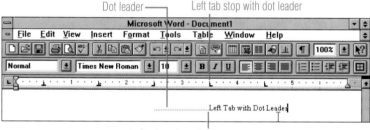

.....................................Left Tab with Dot Leader

Left edge of text lines up with tab stop.

Centering and Justifying Text

Use Word's Alignment feature to change how text is aligned. You can have text centered between margins, aligned along the left or right margins, or justified across both margins. You can align small or large amounts of text.

1 Select text to align.

2 Click the appropriate alignment tool.

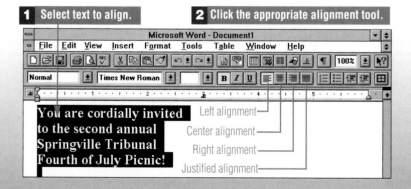

You are cordially invited to the second annual Springville Tribunal Fourth of July Picnic!

Left alignment ——
Center alignment ——
Right alignment ——
Justified alignment ——

Setting Line Spacing

Use Line Spacing to specify how much white space you want between printed lines.

To set a standard line spacing

1 Select the paragraph to apply new spacing to.

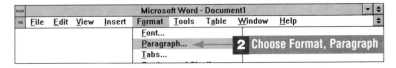

2 Choose Format, Paragraph

3 Pull down the Line Spacing drop-down menu.

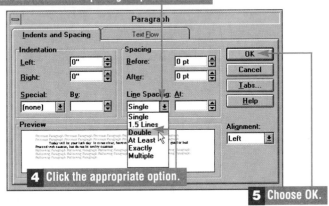

4 Click the appropriate option.

5 Choose OK.

To set customized spacing

1 Select the paragraph to apply new spacing to.

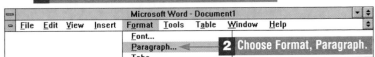

2 Choose Format, Paragraph.

3 Open the Line Spacing drop-down menu.

4 Click the Multiple option.

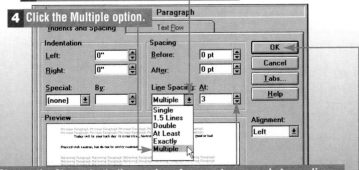

5 Change the At counter to the number of spaces to appear between lines.

6 Choose OK.

AutoFormatting a Document

Word's AutoFormat feature offers a fast and efficient method for formatting an entire document. Headings, paragraphs, lists, and other document elements can be formatting automatically.

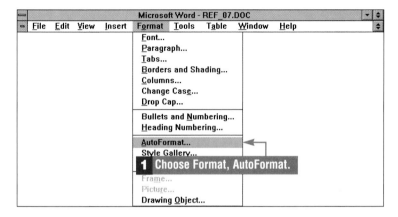

1 Choose Format, AutoFormat.

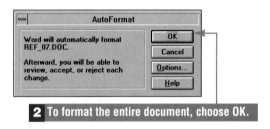

2 To format the entire document, choose OK.

3 Choose Accept to accept the formatting changes.

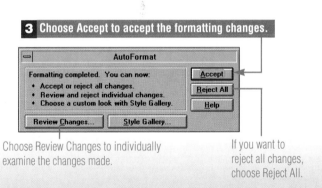

Choose Review Changes to individually examine the changes made.

If you want to reject all changes, choose Reject All.

4 Choose Find to review the changes.

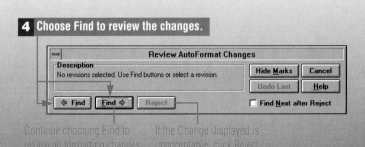

Continue choosing Find to review all formatting changes.

If the Change displayed is unacceptable, click Reject.

Creating Frames

Frames offer a powerful tool for positioning text, tables, graphics, and charts anywhere within a document. Once created, a frame can be positioned so that text flows around it or skips over it.

To create a frame

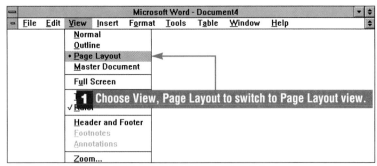

1 Choose View, Page Layout to switch to Page Layout view.

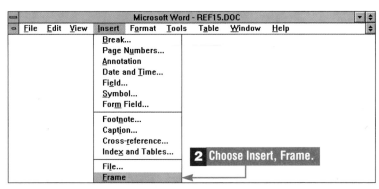

2 Choose Insert, Frame.

3 Move cross hair to where you want upper-left corner of frame to begin.

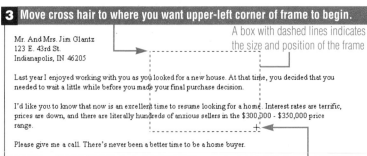

A box with dashed lines indicates the size and position of the frame

4 While depressing the mouse button, drag the cross hair to desired position.

5 Release the mouse button when the size is as you want.

To resize a frame, see "Changing the Graphic's Size."

6 Click the frame's border to select it.

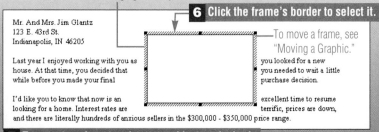

To move a frame, see "Moving a Graphic."

7 Type text, or insert a picture or object as desired.

70

To put a frame around an existing object

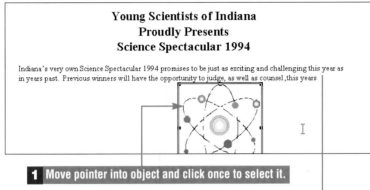

1 Move pointer into object and click once to select it.

To frame existing text, select the text and insert frame.

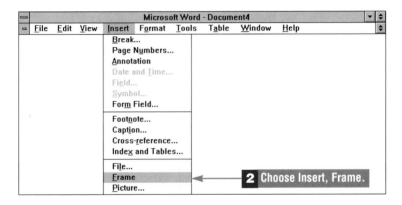

2 Choose Insert, Frame.

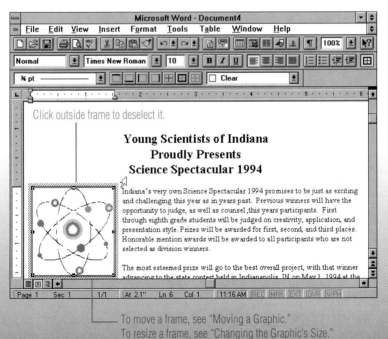

Click outside frame to deselect it.

To move a frame, see "Moving a Graphic."
To resize a frame, see "Changing the Graphic's Size."

Modifying Text Wrapping Around Frames

Putting objects in frames gives you two options on how text outside the frame is arranged around the frame.

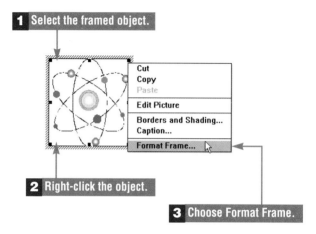

1 Select the framed object.

Cut
Copy
Paste

Edit Picture

Borders and Shading...
Caption...

Format Frame...

2 Right-click the object.

3 Choose Format Frame.

4 Click to choose which type of text wrapping to use.

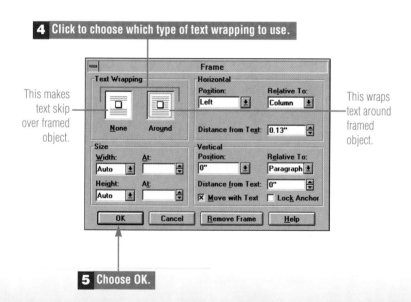

This makes text skip over framed object.

This wraps text around framed object.

5 Choose OK.

Inserting a Graphic Box

Graphics are pre-drawn art that you can insert into Word documents. Some graphics come with Word, and you can buy more graphics—sometimes called *clipart*—from many other sources.

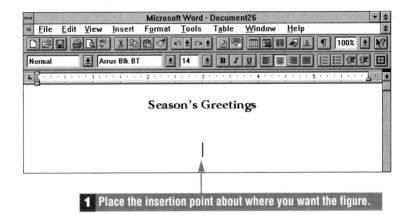

1 Place the insertion point about where you want the figure.

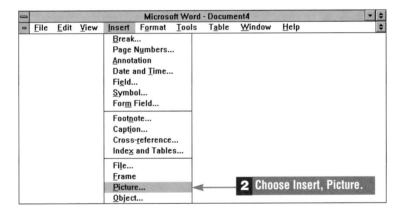

2 Choose Insert, Picture.

3 Select the graphics file you want.

In Word, the clipart files are found in the clipart subdirectory.

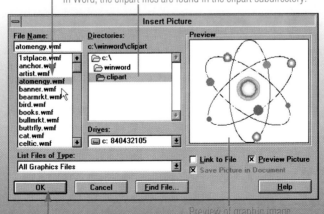

Preview of graphic image

4 Choose OK to insert graphic image into document.

73

Changing the Graphic's Size

Change the size of the graphic or frame to suit the space you have
for it in your document. (See "Creating Frames.")

1 Click the graphic to select it.

Arrow shows which
direction you can drag
handles.

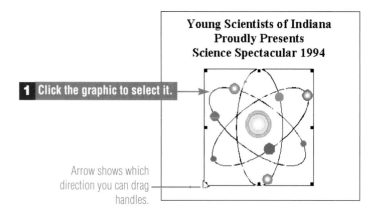

2 Click and hold a handle.

It is easier to use
Page Layout view
when working
with graphics.

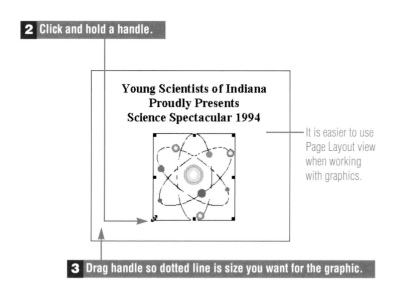

3 Drag handle so dotted line is size you want for the graphic.

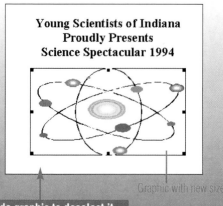

Graphic with new size

4 Click outside graphic to deselect it.

Moving a Graphic

By default, Word puts most graphics at the right side of the page. You can drag a graphic or frame to any position you want in your document. (See "Creating Frames.")

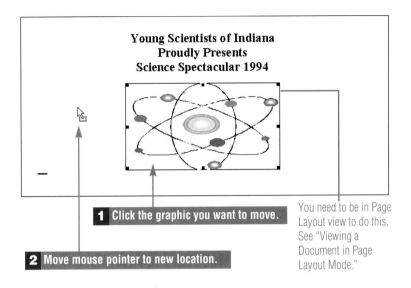

1 Click the graphic you want to move.

You need to be in Page Layout view to do this. See "Viewing a Document in Page Layout Mode."

2 Move mouse pointer to new location.

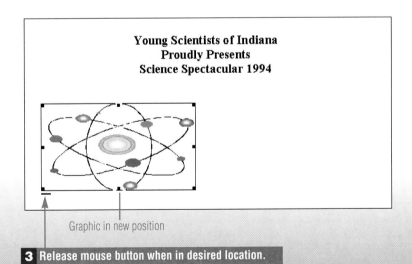

Graphic in new position

3 Release mouse button when in desired location.

Changing the Graphic's Border

Select a border that complements the type of graphic or frame you are using—or you can choose to have no border at all. (See "Creating Frames.")

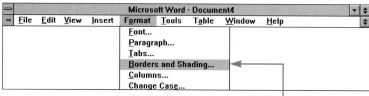

Young Scientists of Indiana
Proudly Presents
Science Spectacular 1994

1 Click once inside graphic.

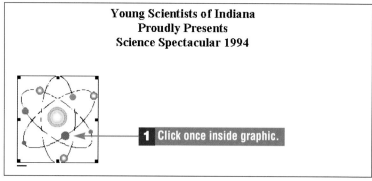

2 Choose Format, Borders and Shading.

3 Choose a pre-designed border.

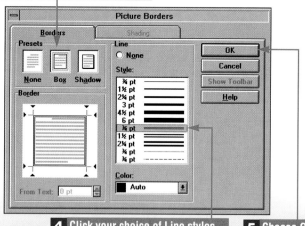

4 Click your choice of Line styles.   **5** Choose OK.

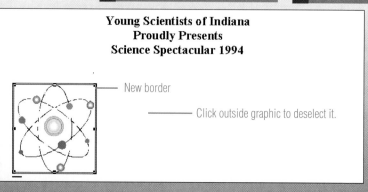

Young Scientists of Indiana
Proudly Presents
Science Spectacular 1994

New border

Click outside graphic to deselect it.

76

Setting a Caption

Use a caption to describe the graphic in your document. The caption is treated as part of the graphic and moves with the graphic.

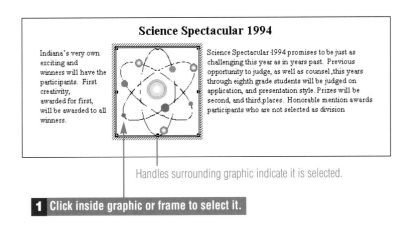

Handles surrounding graphic indicate it is selected.

1 Click inside graphic or frame to select it.

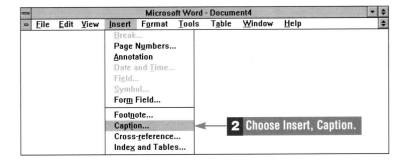

2 Choose Insert, Caption.

3 Type text to be associated with graphic.

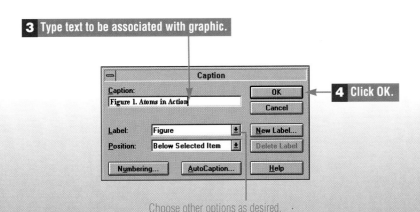

4 Click OK.

Choose other options as desired.

Cropping a Graphic

If you only want to show part of a graphic, you can crop off the undesired portion.

1 Click inside the graphic to select it.

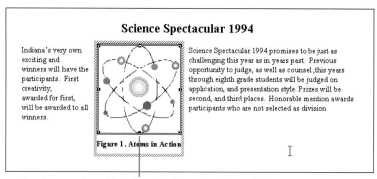

Handles around graphic indicate that it is ready to be modified.

2 Move pointer to handle, hold down Shift and right mouse button.

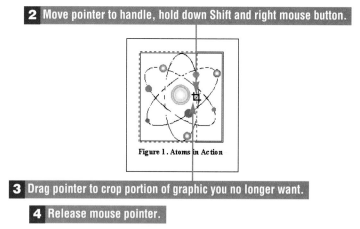

3 Drag pointer to crop portion of graphic you no longer want.

4 Release mouse pointer.

Repeat steps 2-4 to crop other portions of the graphic.

Deleting a Graphic

Deleting a graphic from a document is different from deleting text. You must select the graphic before removing it.

1 Select the graphic you want to delete.

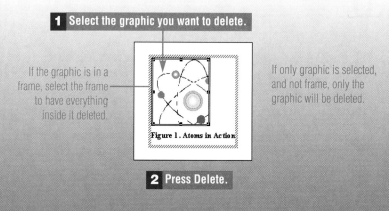

If the graphic is in a frame, select the frame to have everything inside it deleted.

If only graphic is selected, and not frame, only the graphic will be deleted.

2 Press Delete.

78

Searching for Help on a Topic

Use the Search for Help On feature to look up information on how most features in Word work.

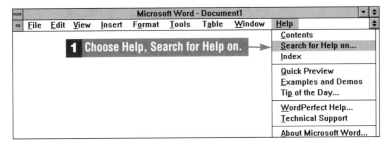

1 Choose Help, Search for Help on.

2 Begin typing the name of the feature you need help on.

The list advances to the available topics as you type.

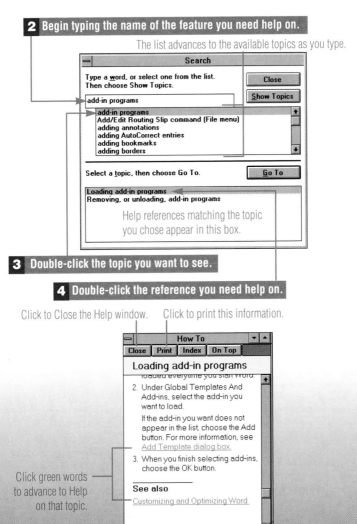

3 Double-click the topic you want to see.

4 Double-click the reference you need help on.

Click to Close the Help window.   Click to print this information.

Click green words to advance to Help on that topic.

Getting Help with Common Tasks

Use the Examples and Demos feature to see a list of common tasks performed in Word.

To use Word's Help menu

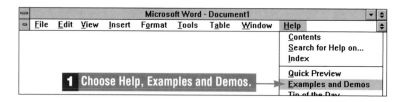

1 Choose Help, Examples and Demos.

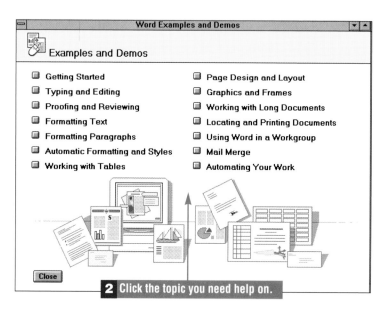

2 Click the topic you need help on.

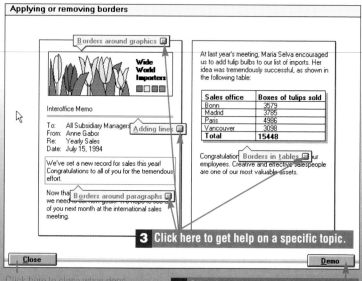

3 Click here to get help on a specific topic.

4 Click here to view a demonstration.

To use the Help button

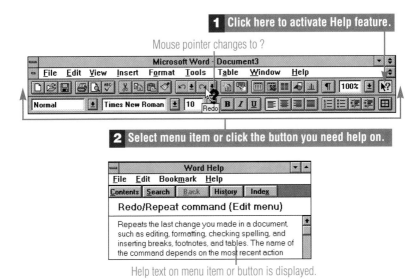

1 Click here to activate Help feature.

Mouse pointer changes to ?

2 Select menu item or click the button you need help on.

Help text on menu item or button is displayed.

Help for WordPerfect Users

If you have recently converted from WordPerfect to Word, Help offers advice on how to simulate WordPerfect tasks.

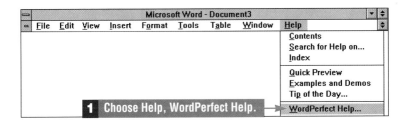

1 Choose Help, WordPerfect Help.

2 Select the WordPerfect topic you need help with.

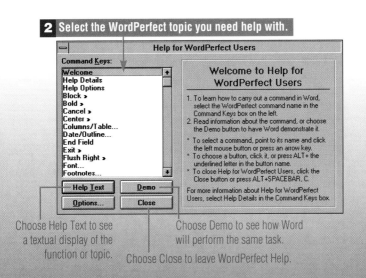

Choose Help Text to see a textual display of the function or topic.

Choose Demo to see how Word will perform the same task.

Choose Close to leave WordPerfect Help.

Viewing a Document and Help Simultaneously

There may be times when you want to work with a document and keep a Help screen visible. With Word, you can experience the best of both worlds.

1 Choose Help, Search for Help on.

2 Double-click the topic you need help with.

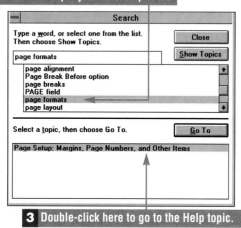

3 Double-click here to go to the Help topic.

4 When the appropriate Help topic is displayed, click On Top.

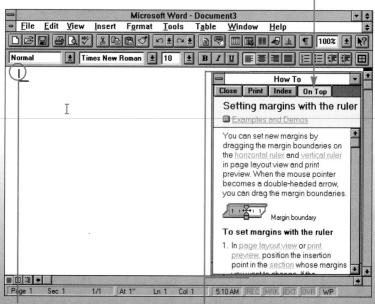

Move the insertion point anywhere in the document and begin or continue editing.

You can refer to the Help window as needed.

Showing, Hiding, and Moving Toolbars

Word has several toolbars available, each containing certain types of commands. You can specify which toolbars you need—and where you need them—at a given time, so you have the commands you need without cluttering the screen.

To show a toolbar

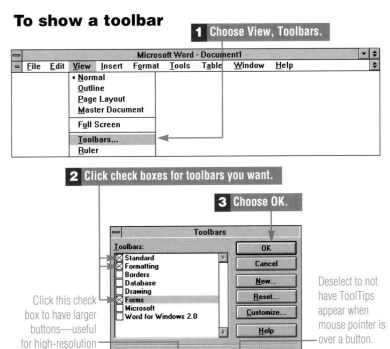

1 Choose View, Toolbars.

2 Click check boxes for toolbars you want.

3 Choose OK.

Click this check box to have larger buttons—useful for high-resolution monitors.

Deselect to not have ToolTips appear when mouse pointer is over a button.

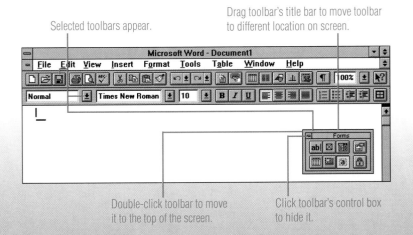

Selected toolbars appear.

Drag toolbar's title bar to move toolbar to different location on screen.

Double-click toolbar to move it to the top of the screen.

Click toolbar's control box to hide it.

83

To hide a toolbar

1 Click right mouse button over toolbar to bring up shortcut menu.

Checked toolbars are currently showing.

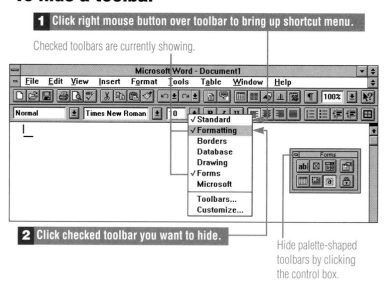

2 Click checked toolbar you want to hide.

Hide palette-shaped
toolbars by clicking
the control box.

To move a toolbar

1 Click in area of bar that is not covered with a button.

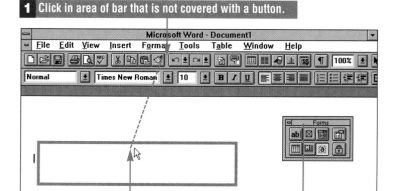

2 Drag toolbar outline to new location.

Click title bar and drag to move palette-shaped toolbars.

Toolbar becomes floating palette.

Drag toolbar palette to any edge of window to make it a bar again.

Double-click toolbar's title bar to move it back to top of window.

Creating a Toolbar

Create new toolbars to hold sets of commands you use frequently. You can show these toolbars when you need them and hide them when you want more space on the screen. See "To show a toolbar" and "To hide a toolbar."

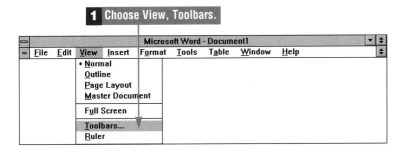

1 Choose View, Toolbars.

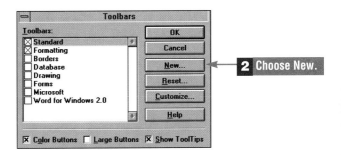

2 Choose New.

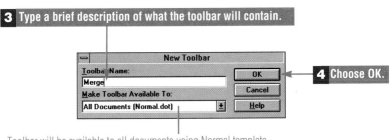

3 Type a brief description of what the toolbar will contain.

4 Choose OK.

Toolbar will be available to all documents using Normal template.

more ▶

5 See "Editing a Toolbar" to add buttons to the new toolbar.

New toolbar, before buttons are added.

6 When finished adding buttons, choose Close.

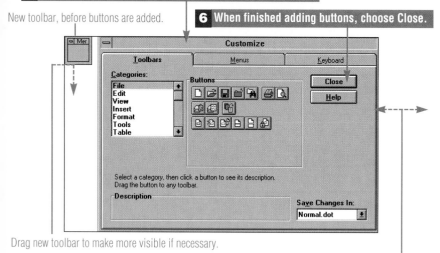

Drag new toolbar to make more visible if necessary.

Move dialog box to give more room to toolbar, if necessary.

7 Double-click title bar to move toolbar to top of window.

Click control box to hide toolbar.

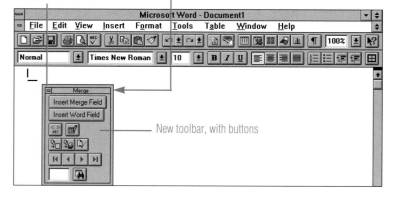

New toolbar, with buttons

New toolbar at top of window with other toolbars.

Customizing a Toolbar

Word comes with several pre-defined toolbars, each holding specific buttons. You can add buttons you need and remove buttons you don't use, in order to make finding the commands you need faster and easier.

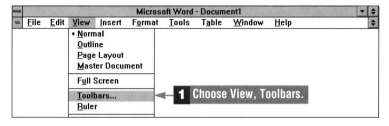

1 Choose View, Toolbars.

2 Check any toolbars you want to customize.

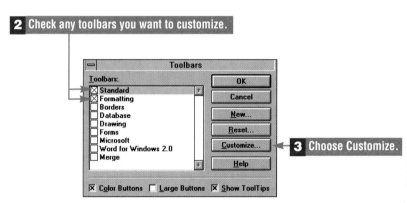

3 Choose Customize.

4 See "Editing a Toolbar" to add and remove buttons.

5 When finished changing the toolbars, choose Close.

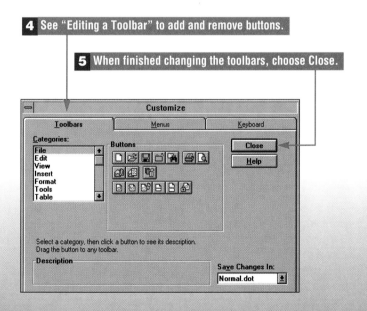

Editing a Toolbar

Add buttons you need to a toolbar, and remove buttons you don't use. You can also change the position of buttons on the toolbar. You can edit toolbars you create yourself, as well as toolbars included with Word.

To add a button to a toolbar

1 See "Creating a Toolbar" or "Customizing a Toolbar" to get to this dialog box.

2 Click a general category of commands.

3 Click the button you want on a toolbar.

4 Drag button to where you want it on toolbar.

5 Repeat steps 2-4 to add other buttons. Other buttons move to make room for new button.

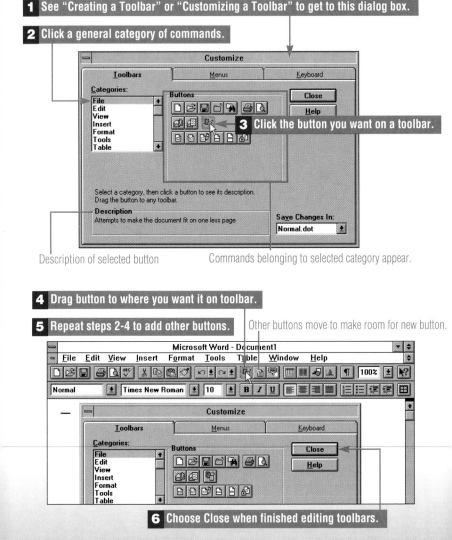

Description of selected button

Commands belonging to selected category appear.

6 Choose Close when finished editing toolbars.

To move a button to a different place on the toolbar

1 See "Creating a Toolbar" or "Customizing a Toolbar" to get to this dialog box.

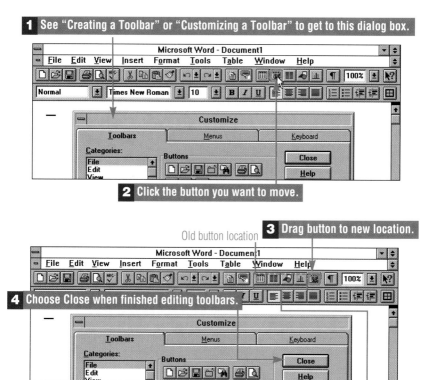

2 Click the button you want to move.

Old button location   **3** Drag button to new location.

4 Choose Close when finished editing toolbars.

Buttons in toolbar adjust to make room for new button location.

To remove buttons from a toolbar

1 See "Creating a Toolbar" or "Customizing a Toolbar" to get to this dialog box.

2 Click the button you want to remove.

3 Drag button from toolbar into document area.

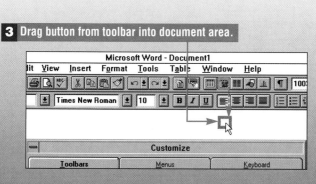

4 Repeat steps 2-3 to remove other buttons.

Toolbar automatically closes gap where button was located.

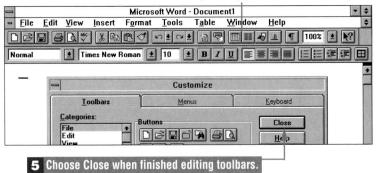

5 Choose Close when finished editing toolbars.

To make space between buttons in a toolbar

1 See "Creating a Toolbar" or "Customizing a Toolbar" to get to this dialog box.

Need space between these two buttons.

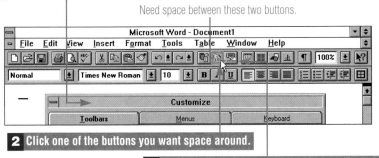

2 Click one of the buttons you want space around.

3 Drag very short distance away from other button.

Space created between buttons.

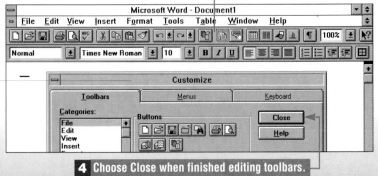

4 Choose Close when finished editing toolbars.

Customizing Menus

Add frequently used commands to Word's menus to make access quicker. You also can remove unused commands.

1 Choose Tools, Customize.

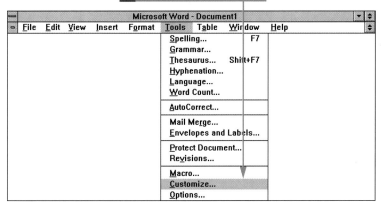

2 Choose the Menus tab.

3 Click the category of commands you want to see.

List of commands in selected category

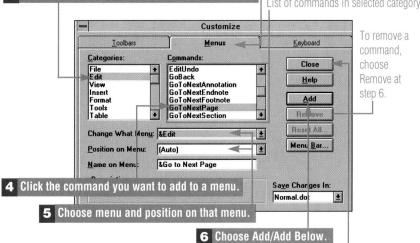

To remove a command, choose Remove at step 6.

4 Click the command you want to add to a menu.

5 Choose menu and position on that menu.

6 Choose Add/Add Below.

7 Choose Close when finished adding menu items.

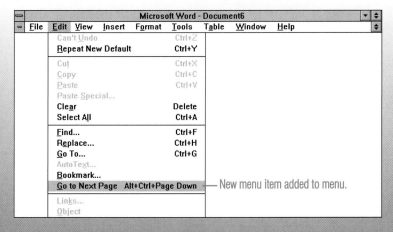

New menu item added to menu.

Adding a Menu

You can add menus to the menu bar. The new menu can contain commands you use often that are not contained in other menus.

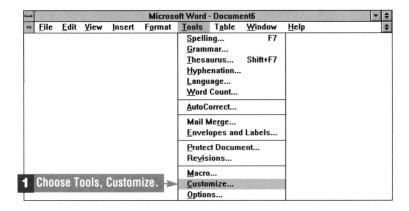

1 Choose Tools, Customize.

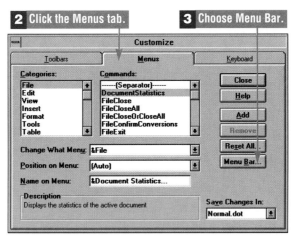

2 Click the Menus tab.

3 Choose Menu Bar.

4 Type name for menu.

Put & symbol before mnemonic character (character to be underlined).

6 Choose Add/Add After.

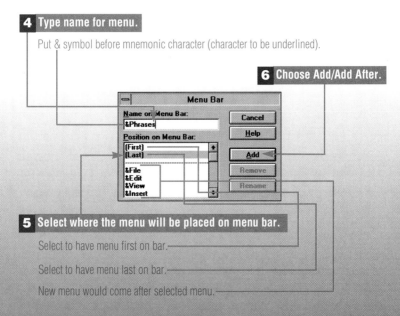

5 Select where the menu will be placed on menu bar.

Select to have menu first on bar.

Select to have menu last on bar.

New menu would come after selected menu.

7 Follow steps 2-11 in "Customizing Menus" to add items to new menu.

New menu added to list of menus.

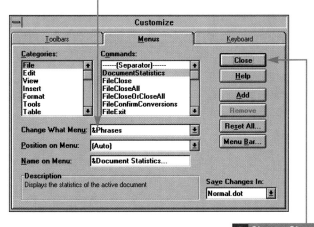

8 Choose Close.

Customizing the Keyboard

Specify keystroke combinations to quickly perform commands you use frequently.

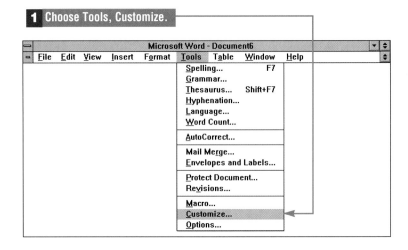

1 Choose Tools, Customize.

2 Click Keyboard tab.

3 Click category of commands you want to see.

4 Click command you want assigned to a keystroke.

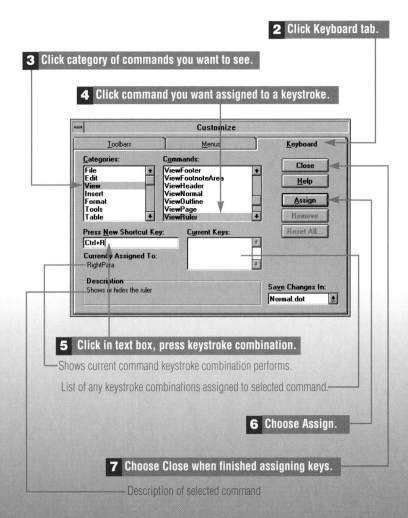

5 Click in text box, press keystroke combination.

Shows current command keystroke combination performs.

List of any keystroke combinations assigned to selected command.

6 Choose Assign.

7 Choose Close when finished assigning keys.

Description of selected command

Recording Macros

A macro is a series of commands and/or text you use frequently. By recording macros, you can have Word perform these tasks quickly and efficiently. You can have a list of macros you use, as well as assign macros to menus, toolbars, and keystroke combinations. You play the macro just by choosing it from a menu, clicking a button, or pressing a keystroke.

To record a macro

New documents are good for recording macros.

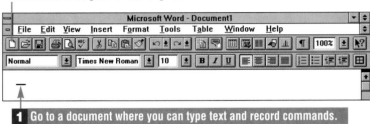

1 Go to a document where you can type text and record commands.

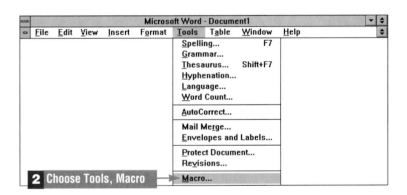

2 Choose Tools, Macro

3 Type a name for the macro.

Spaces aren't allowed in the macro name.

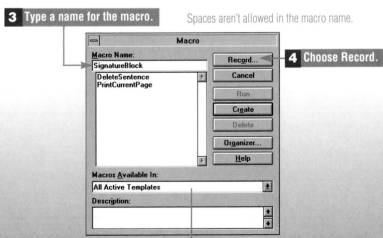

4 Choose Record.

Macro will be accessible from documents based on NORMAL.DOT.

5 Type a brief description of what the macro will do.

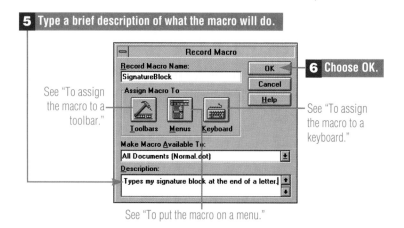

See "To assign the macro to a toolbar."

6 Choose OK.

See "To assign the macro to a keyboard."

See "To put the macro on a menu."

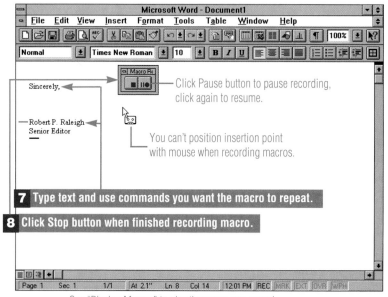

Click Pause button to pause recording, click again to resume.

You can't position insertion point with mouse when recording macros.

7 Type text and use commands you want the macro to repeat.

8 Click Stop button when finished recording macro.

See "Playing Macros" to play the macro you record.

To assign the macro to a toolbar

1 Follow steps 1-5 in "To record a macro."

2 Choose Toolbars.

3 Click macro name.

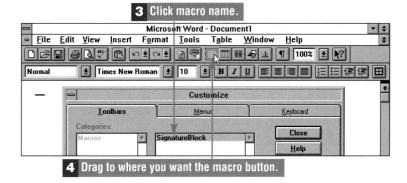

4 Drag to where you want the macro button.

5 Click icon you want button to look like.

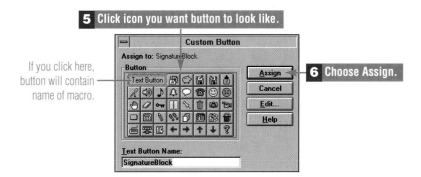

If you click here, button will contain name of macro.

6 Choose Assign.

New button

7 Choose Close.

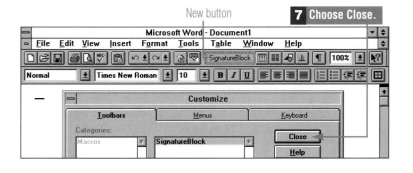

8 Type text and use commands you want macro to repeat.

9 When finished recording macro, click Stop button.

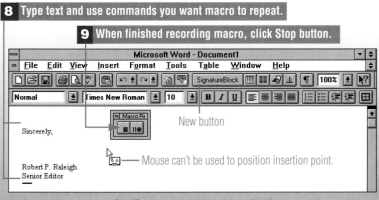

New button

Mouse can't be used to position insertion point.

See "To play a macro from the toolbar."

To put the macro on a menu

1 Follow steps 1-5 in "To record a macro."

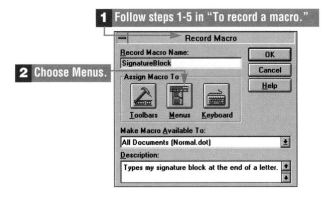

2 Choose Menus.

Record Macro

Record Macro Name:
SignatureBlock

Assign Macro To
Toolbars Menus Keyboard

Make Macro Available To:
All Documents (Normal.dot)

Description:
Types my signature block at the end of a letter.

OK
Cancel
Help

3 Choose menu and position on menu.

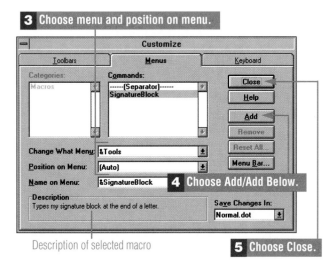

Customize

Toolbars   Menus   Keyboard

Categories: Commands:
Macros   ------(Separator)------
               SignatureBlock

Close
Help
Add
Remove
Reset All
Menu Bar...

Change What Menu: &Tools
Position on Menu: (Auto)
Name on Menu: &SignatureBlock   **4** Choose Add/Add Below.

Description
Types my signature block at the end of a letter.

Save Changes In:
Normal.dot

Description of selected macro

5 Choose Close.

6 Type text and use commands you want macro to repeat.

See "To play a macro from the menu."

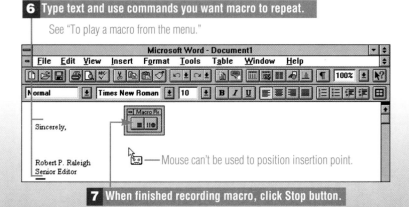

Microsoft Word - Document1

File Edit View Insert Format Tools Table Window Help

Normal   Times New Roman   10   B I U   100%

Sincerely,

Robert P. Raleigh
Senior Editor

Macro Re

— Mouse can't be used to position insertion point.

7 When finished recording macro, click Stop button.

To assign the macro to a keyboard

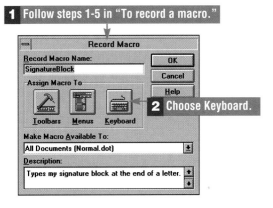

1 Follow steps 1-5 in "To record a macro."

2 Choose Keyboard.

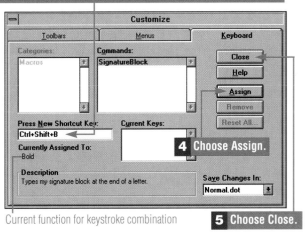

3 Press keystroke combination you want to activate the macro.

4 Choose Assign.

Current function for keystroke combination

5 Choose Close.

6 Type text and use commands you want macro to repeat.

7 When finished recording macro, Click Stop button.

Mouse can't be used to position insertion point.

See "To play a macro from the keyboard."

Playing Macros

Once you have created a macro, you can play it whenever you need that text and/or commands in your document. How you play the macro depends on how you recorded it.

To play a macro from the Macro dialog box

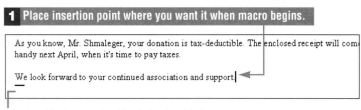

1 Place insertion point where you want it when macro begins.

As you know, Mr. Shmaleger, your donation is tax-deductible. The enclosed receipt will come handy next April, when it's time to pay taxes.

We look forward to your continued association and support.

Signature block macro should put signature block here.

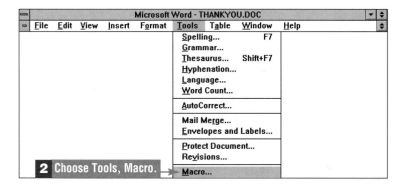

Microsoft Word - THANKYOU.DOC

| File | Edit | View | Insert | Format | Tools | Table | Window | Help |

Spelling...   F7
Grammar...
Thesaurus...   Shift+F7
Hyphenation...
Language...
Word Count...

AutoCorrect...

Mail Merge...
Envelopes and Labels...

Protect Document...
Revisions...

2 Choose Tools, Macro. → Macro...

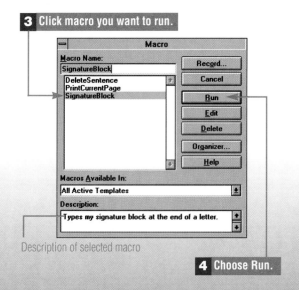

3 Click macro you want to run.

Macro

Macro Name:
SignatureBlock

DeleteSentence
PrintCurrentPage
SignatureBlock

Record...
Cancel
Run
Edit
Delete
Organizer...
Help

Macros Available In:
All Active Templates

Description:
Types my signature block at the end of a letter.

Description of selected macro

4 Choose Run.

To play a macro from the toolbar

1 Place insertion point where you want it when macro begins.

2 Click macro button.

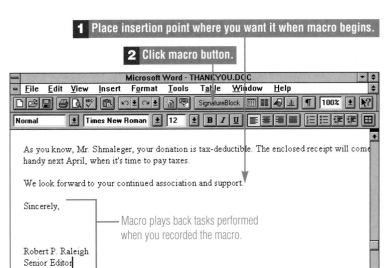

As you know, Mr. Shmaleger, your donation is tax-deductible. The enclosed receipt will come handy next April, when it's time to pay taxes.

We look forward to your continued association and support.

Sincerely,

Macro plays back tasks performed when you recorded the macro.

Robert P. Raleigh
Senior Editor

To play a macro from the keyboard

1 Place insertion point where you want it when macro begins.

As you know, Mr. Shmaleger, your donation is tax-deductible. The enclosed receipt will come handy next April, when it's time to pay taxes.

We look forward to your continued association and support.

Signature block macro should put signature block here.

2 Press keystroke combination used when recording macro.

As you know, Mr. Shmaleger, your donation is tax-deductible. The enclosed receipt will come handy next April, when it's time to pay taxes.

We look forward to your continued association and support.

Sincerely,

Macro plays back tasks performed when you recorded the macro.

Robert P. Raleigh
Senior Editor

To play a macro from the menu

1 Place insertion point where you want it when macro begins.

> detailing the important events around the world, the nation and our fair town.
>
> As you know, Mr. Shmaleger, your donation is tax-deductible. The enclosed receipt will come
> handy next April, when it's time to pay taxes.
>
> We look forward to your continued association and support.

Signature block macro should
put signature block here.

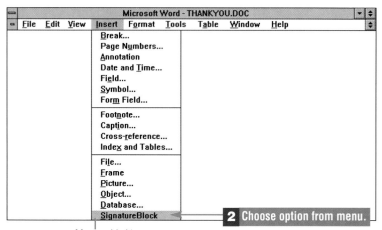

Macro added to menu

2 Choose option from menu.

> As you know, Mr. Shmaleger, your donation is tax-deductible. The enclosed receipt will come
> handy next April, when it's time to pay taxes.
>
> We look forward to your continued association and support.
>
> Sincerely,
>
> Robert P. Raleigh
> Senior Editor

Macro plays back tasks performed
when you recorded the macro.

Creating the Main Document

Mail Merge lets you create form letters with customized information for each recipient. A mail merge has two parts: the main document and the data source. The main document is the letter itself, with codes called *fields* indicating where information from the data source should be inserted.

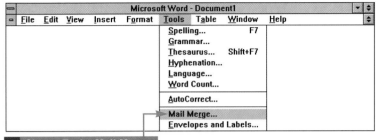

1 Choose Tools, Mail Merge.

2 Click Create to see drop-down menu.

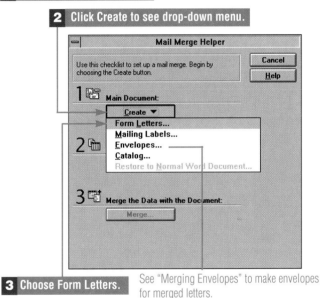

3 Choose Form Letters. See "Merging Envelopes" to make envelopes for merged letters.

4 Choose New Main Document

Choose Active Window if starting from a blank screen or a letter you want to use.

more ▶

103

Mail Merge: Creating Form Letters

5 Choose Get Data to see drop-down menu.

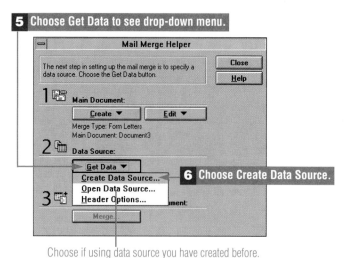

6 Choose Create Data Source.

Choose if using data source you have created before.

7 Type information type, choose Add Field Name to add to list.

You can't use spaces in field names.

List of types of custom information to be included in mail merge letters.

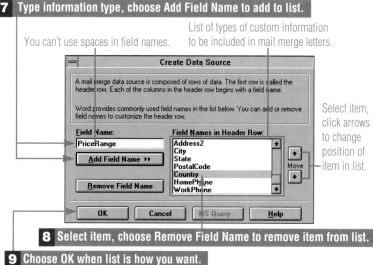

Select item, click arrows to change position of item in list.

8 Select item, choose Remove Field Name to remove item from list.

9 Choose OK when list is how you want.

Repeat steps 7 and 8 until the list contains types of information you want.

10 Change to directory where you want the data source saved.

11 Type file name for data source.

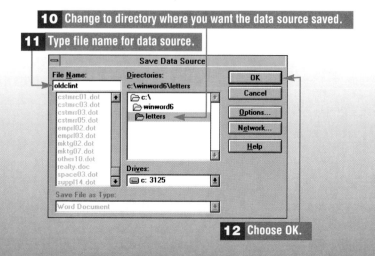

12 Choose OK.

13 Choose Edit Main Document to create form letter.

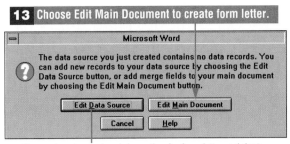

Choose to enter custom information for form letter recipients.

14 Type letter normally.

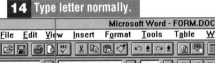

Mail Merge toolbar

Recipient's title will be inserted at insertion point.

15 When letter needs custom information, choose Insert Merge Field.

16 Choose type of information to be inserted in letter.

These merge codes will insert recipient's address.
Insert spaces between merge codes and words.
Remember to save document frequently.

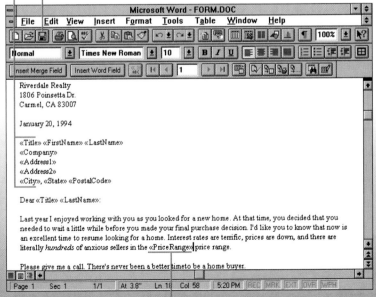

This merge code will insert recipient's home price range.

17 See "Creating the Data Source" to type recipients' custom information.

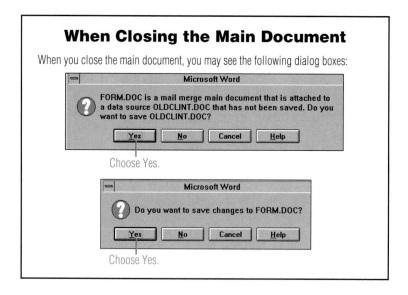

When Closing the Main Document

When you close the main document, you may see the following dialog boxes:

Choose Yes.

Choose Yes.

Creating the Data Source

A mail merge has two parts: the main document and the data source. The data source contains specific information—such as names, addresses, and phone numbers—for each of the people included in the merge.

If main document (form letter) is already open, skip to step 5.

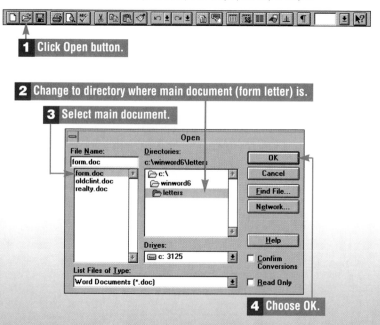

1 Click Open button.

2 Change to directory where main document (form letter) is.

3 Select main document.

4 Choose OK.

5 Choose Edit Data Source button.

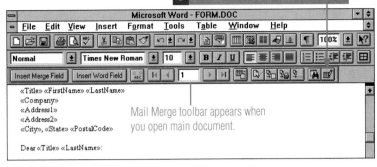

Mail Merge toolbar appears when you open main document.

6 Type information for one person, pressing Enter after each item.

See first record.

See previous record.

Leave text box blank if information type doesn't apply.

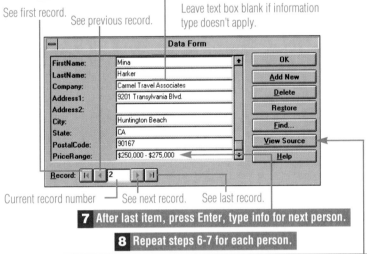

Current record number

See next record.

See last record.

7 After last item, press Enter, type info for next person.

8 Repeat steps 6-7 for each person.

9 Choose View Source when finished entering info for all people.

10 Choose Save button to save data.

11 Double-click to close normally.

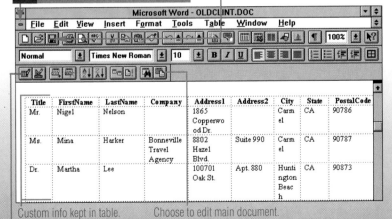

Custom info kept in table.   Choose to edit main document.

Choose Edit Data Source to add more records.

12 See "Merging the Document" to merge with main document.

Merging the Document

After you have created the main document and the data source, you can merge the two together to have a personalized letter for each recipient.

Skip to step 5 if the Main document is already open.

1 Choose the Open button.

2 Change to the directory containing the main document.

3 Select the main document.

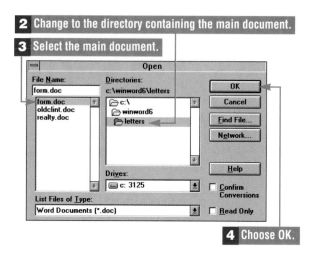

4 Choose OK.

5 Choose Merge to New Document button.

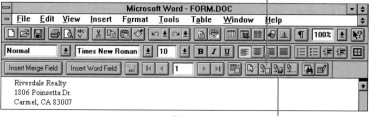

Click here to send documents directly to printer.

Break between each letter

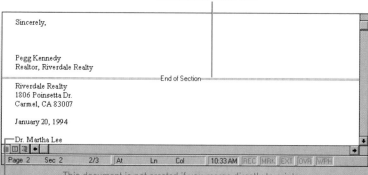

This document is not created if you merge directly to printer.

Custom information in each letter

Merging Envelopes

You may want to create envelopes for the form letters made with mail merge. You can use the same data source file to create envelopes for each of the letters.

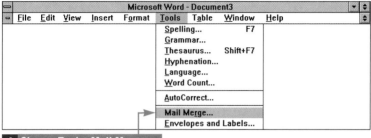

1 Choose Tools, Mail Merge.

2 Choose Create to see drop-down menu.

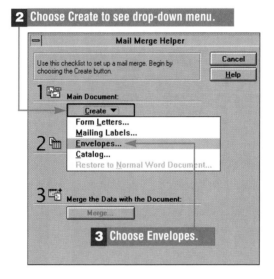

3 Choose Envelopes.

Choose Active Window if the current window is empty.

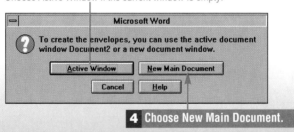

4 Choose New Main Document.

more ▶

109

5 Click Get Data to see drop-down menu.

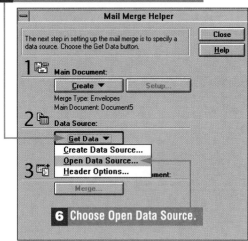

6 Choose Open Data Source.

7 Select directory containing data source file.

8 Select data source filename.

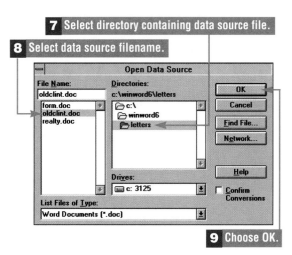

9 Choose OK.

10 Choose Set Up Main Document.

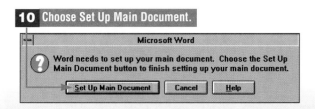

Preview of envelope size and address placement

Click if not using standard-sized envelopes.

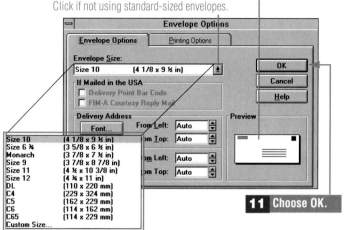

11 Choose OK.

Choose the size of envelope you're using.

12 Click to see list of field names.

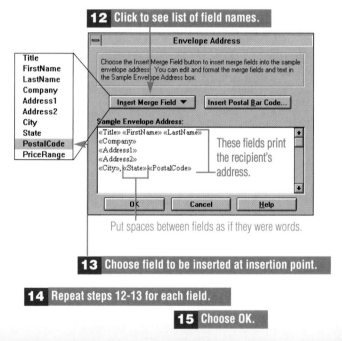

These fields print the recipient's address.

Put spaces between fields as if they were words.

13 Choose field to be inserted at insertion point.

14 Repeat steps 12-13 for each field.

15 Choose OK.

more ▶

111

16 Choose Edit to see drop-down menu.

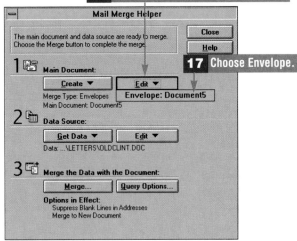

17 Choose Envelope.

18 Type a return address, if not using pre-printed envelopes.

Choose to merge straight to printer.

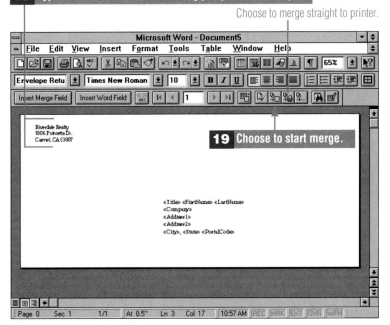

19 Choose to start merge.

Setting Margins

Change the white space around the text on the page. Increase margin size for more white space, decrease margin size to allow for more text.

1 Place insertion point on page to view margins in Print Preview.

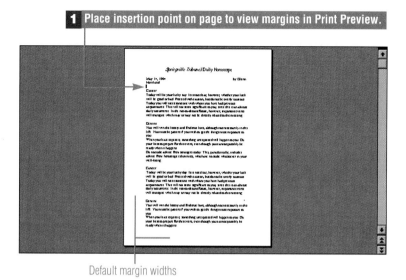

Default margin widths

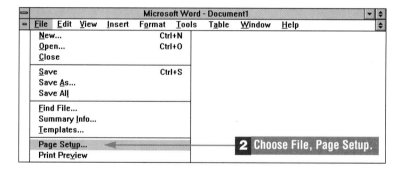

2 Choose File, Page Setup.

3 Click Margins tab.

Preview of how page will look with new margins

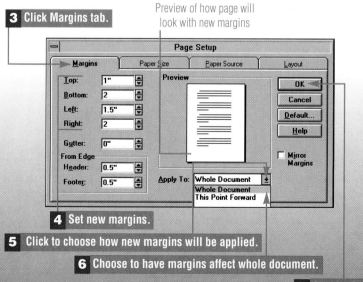

4 Set new margins.

5 Click to choose how new margins will be applied.

6 Choose to have margins affect whole document.

7 Choose OK.

Centering Text Between Top and Bottom Margins

Center text between the top and bottom margins of a page when you are creating a title page or want other text centered vertically on the page.

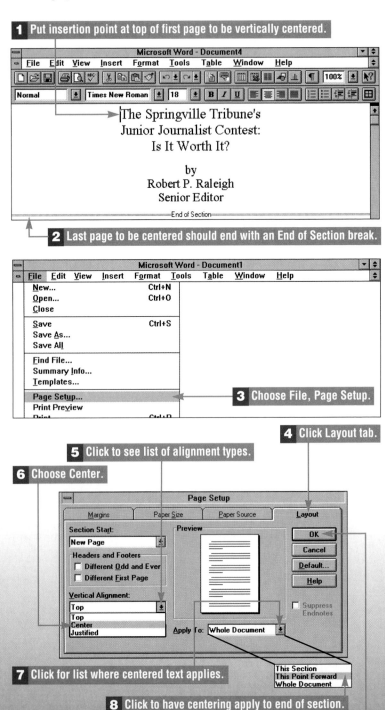

1 Put insertion point at top of first page to be vertically centered.

2 Last page to be centered should end with an End of Section break.

3 Choose File, Page Setup.

4 Click Layout tab.

5 Click to see list of alignment types.

6 Choose Center.

7 Click for list where centered text applies.

8 Click to have centering apply to end of section.

9 Choose OK.

Page Numbering

Page numbering puts the current page number at a specified
location on each page in the document.

1 Move insertion point to first page you want page numbering.

Page numbering will go here.

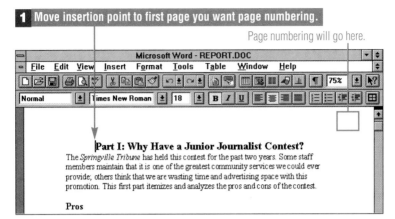

2 Choose Insert, Page Numbers.

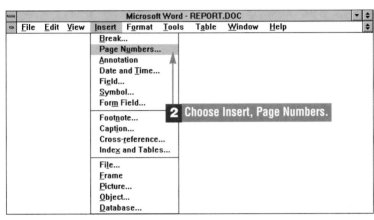

3 Click for vertical placement of page number.

Preview of where
page number goes.

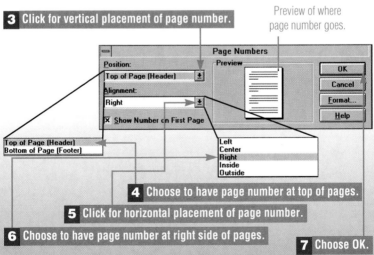

4 Choose to have page number at top of pages.

5 Click for horizontal placement of page number.

6 Choose to have page number at right side of pages.

7 Choose OK.

Creating Headers and Footers

Headers and footers are text that appear at the top or bottom of each page in the document. Headers appear above the document's body text; footers appear below the body text.

1 Place insertion point in page where you want header or footer.

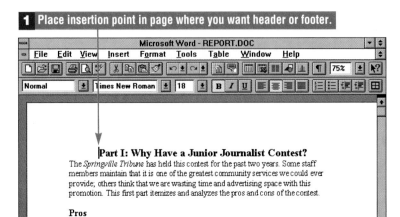

2 Choose View, Header and Footer.

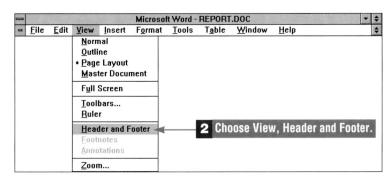

3 Type information in header or footer.

Insert page number.   Insert time.

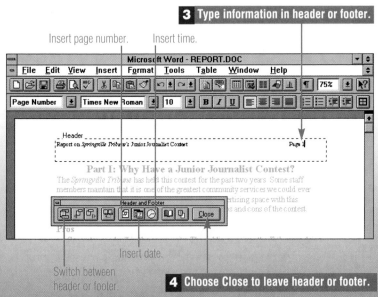

Insert date.

Switch between header or footer.

4 Choose Close to leave header or footer.

Setting a paper size

Set a paper size when you want to print on a different size of paper—such as legal—or when you want to print landscape (sideways) on the page.

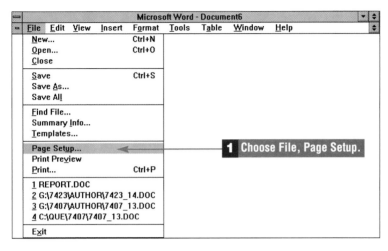

1 Choose File, Page Setup.

2 Click Paper Size tab.

3 Click to see list of paper sizes.

Click Landscape for sideways printing.

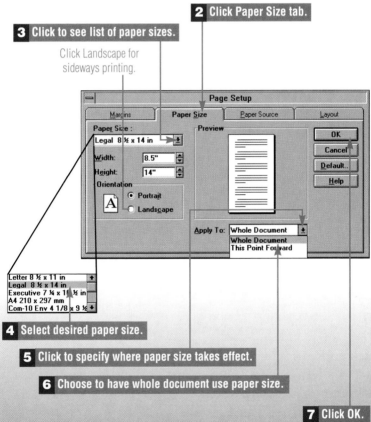

4 Select desired paper size.

5 Click to specify where paper size takes effect.

6 Choose to have whole document use paper size.

7 Click OK.

Creating Newspaper Columns

Use columns to make text wrap in columns, like in newspapers and magazines. This is useful especially for creating newsletters.

1 Place insertion point where columns should begin.

2 Click Columns button.

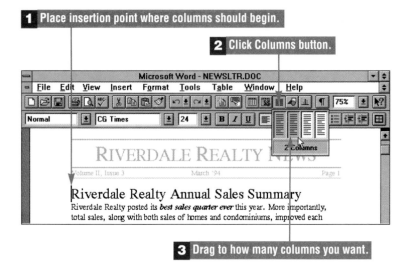

3 Drag to how many columns you want.

Text flows into columns.

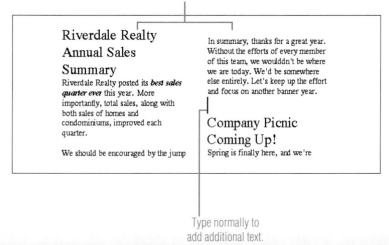

Type normally to
add additional text.

Printing the Whole Document

When you need to see the document on paper, use Word's print feature to print the entire document. See "Printing One Page" and "Printing Several Pages" for when you want to print parts of the document.

1 Click the Print button to print the entire document.

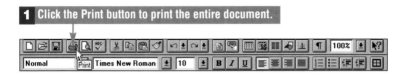

Printing One Page of the Document

Use this feature when you need to print only one page from the document.

1 Place insertion point in the page you want to print.

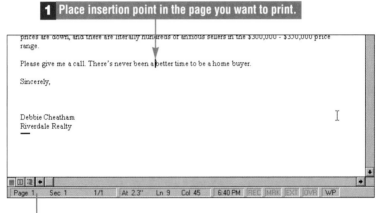

Check status bar to see if you are on the correct page.

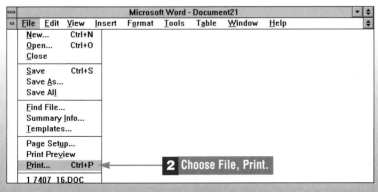

2 Choose File, Print.

more ▶

119

3 Click Current Page.

Print

Printer:	HP LaserJet IIISi on QUE_02/HPIIISI

Print What: Document

Copies: 1

Page Range
- ○ All
- ● Current Page ○ Selection
- ○ Pages:

Enter page numbers and/or page ranges
separated by commas. For example, 1,3,5-12

Print: All Pages in Range

OK

Cancel

Options...

Printer...

Help

☐ Print to File

☒ Collate Copies

4 Choose OK to print.

Printing Several Pages

When you need to print some, but not all, of the pages in a
document, use the Print Multiple Pages feature.

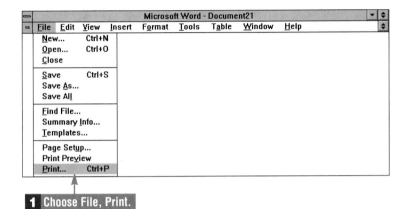

1 Choose File, Print.

2 Click Pages.

Prints pages 1 through 3.

Prints pages 5 and 8.

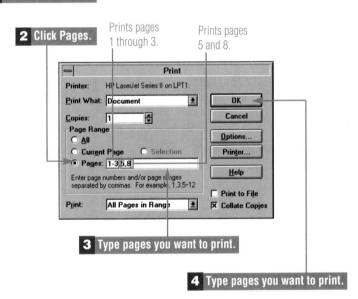

3 Type pages you want to print.

4 Type pages you want to print.

121

Printing a Document on Disk

You can print a document you don't currently have open by using the print command from the Find File dialog box.

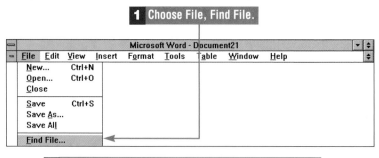

1 Choose File, Find File.

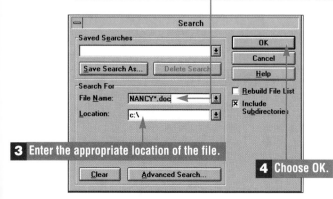

2 Enter any search criteria for the file you wish to print.

3 Enter the appropriate location of the file.

4 Choose OK.

5 Select the file you want to print.

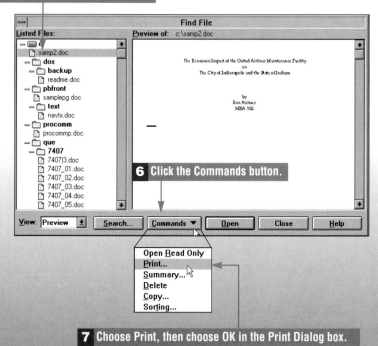

6 Click the Commands button.

7 Choose Print, then choose OK in the Print Dialog box.

Printing an Envelope

Use Word's Envelope feature to print envelopes for letters you have written.

To create an envelope

1 Choose Tools, Envelopes and Labels.

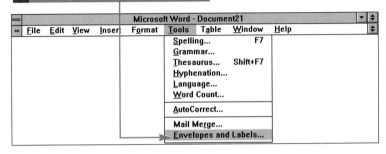

2 Accept the default Delivery Address, or type a new Delivery Address.

3 Accept the default Return Address, or type a new one.

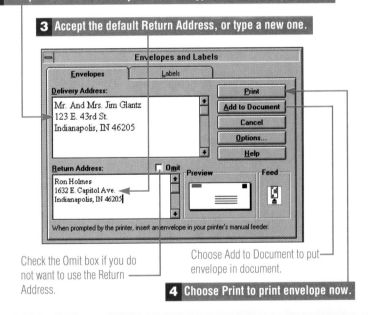

Check the Omit box if you do not want to use the Return Address.

Choose Add to Document to put envelope in document.

4 Choose Print to print envelope now.

123

To include a POSTNET bar code with envelope

1 See steps 1-3 in "Printing an Envelope" to insert envelope information.

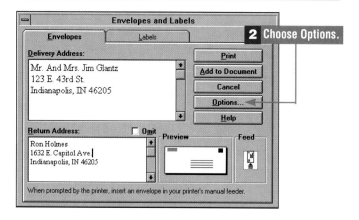

2 Choose Options.

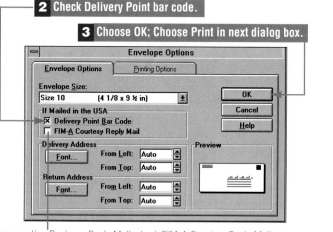

2 Check Delivery Point bar code.

3 Choose OK; Choose Print in next dialog box.

If you are creating Business Reply Mail, check FIM-A Courtesy Reply Mail.

Printing Labels

Word's Labels feature lets you print on a wide variety of adhesive labels. It is important to note here that Word's Envelope and Label feature only allows you to print a single label at a time or multiple labels with the same address.

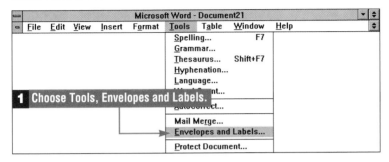

1 Choose Tools, Envelopes and Labels.

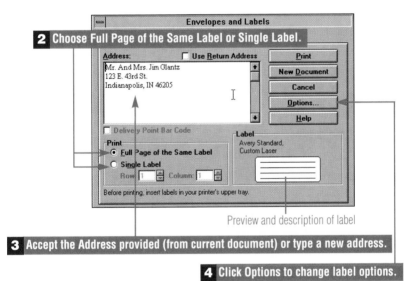

2 Choose Full Page of the Same Label or Single Label.

Preview and description of label

3 Accept the Address provided (from current document) or type a new address.

4 Click Options to change label options.

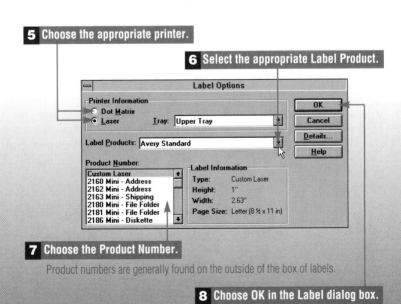

5 Choose the appropriate printer.

6 Select the appropriate Label Product.

7 Choose the Product Number.

Product numbers are generally found on the outside of the box of labels.

8 Choose OK in the Label dialog box.

125

Checking Spelling

Use the Speller to find typos and misspelled words. Be sure to proofread your text yourself though; it's possible to type something that is a real word, but not the correct word—such as typing *reality* instead of *Realty*.

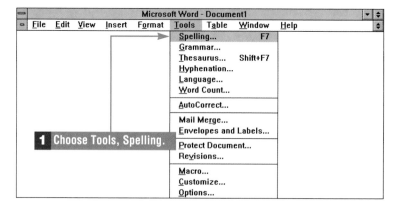

1 Choose Tools, Spelling.

2 Scroll through list of suggestions.

Spellcheck finds the first misspelled word.

Suggestions to replace misspelled word.

3 Select correct spelling.

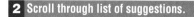

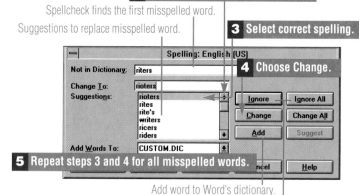

4 Choose Change.

5 Repeat steps 3 and 4 for all misspelled words.

Add word to Word's dictionary.

Choose Ignore or Ignore All to ignore other occurrences of the word.

Box appears when spellcheck is finished.

> **Microsoft Word**
> 🛈 The spelling check is complete.
> [OK]

6 Choose OK.

To check part of a document

Most of our articles and columns are done by staff riters and freelancers. This work is likely to come in in a lot of different formats, making the editors perform many formatting and file conversion tasks, instead of the work ther're best at. The Springville Tribunal Authoring System will help fix this mess. By using the authoring system, many of the mundane aspects of each job will be handled automatically, letting all parties in the process concentrate more on things that require intelligence

1 Select text that you want to spellcheck.

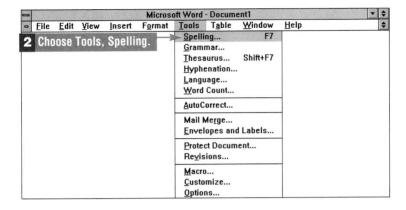

To customize the spellcheck

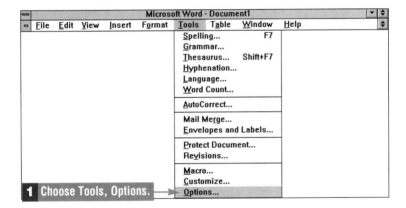

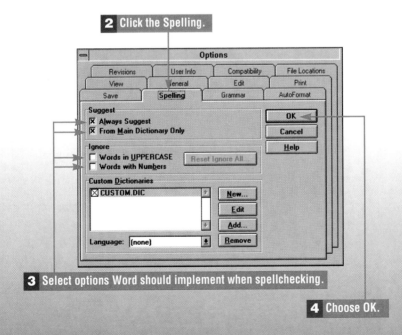

Looking Up Words with the Thesaurus

Use the thesaurus to look up synonyms and antonyms of words in your document. The thesaurus can replace the old word with the word you choose.

1 Place insertion point in word you want to look up.

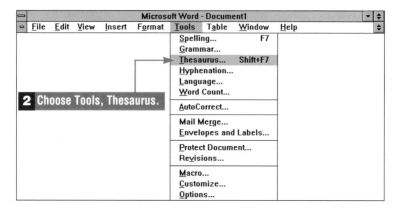

2 Choose Tools, Thesaurus.

3 Select the appropriate meaning, or choose Antonyms.

4 Choose Replace to change the selected word.

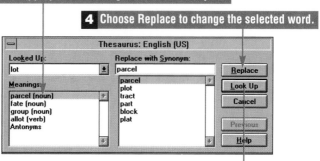

Use Look Up to look up a word in the Replace with Synonym box.

Most of our articles and columns are done by staff riters and freelancers. This work is likely to come in in a block of different formats, making the editors perform many formatting and file conversion tasks, instead of the work ther're best at. The Springville Tribune Authoring System will help fix this mess. By using the authoring system, many of the mundane aspects of each job will be handled automatically, letting all parties in the process concentrate more on things that require intelligence.

Word replaced by thesaurus.

Using the Grammar Feature

The Grammar feature analyzes your document for rules of grammar, as well as sentence length and readability.

1 Place insertion point anywhere in document.

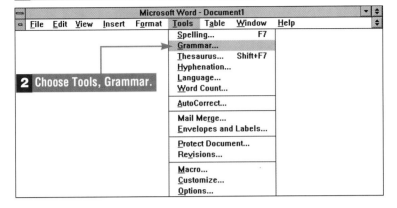

2 Choose Tools, Grammar.

Choose the Next Sentence button to skip the current sentence.

Choose the Ignore button to ignore the suggestion.

3 Select text within Sentence box.

Sentence with grammatical error is displayed here.

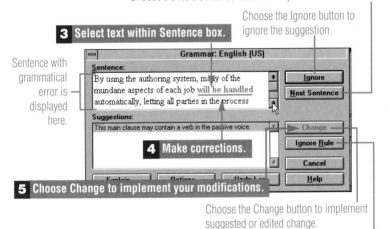

4 Make corrections.

5 Choose Change to implement your modifications.

Choose the Change button to implement suggested or edited change.

Choose the Ignore Rules button to ignore the grammar rule for remainder of grammar check.

Word displays summary of grammar check statistics.

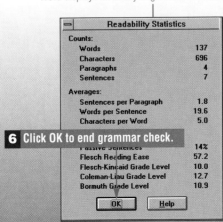

6 Click OK to end grammar check.

Correcting Errors as You Type

With Word's AutoCorrect feature, common typing mistakes are recognized and corrected as you type. AutoCorrect also is capable of substituting lengthy phrases by recognizing abbreviations you have defined.

To add AutoCorrect entries through the AutoCorrect dialog box

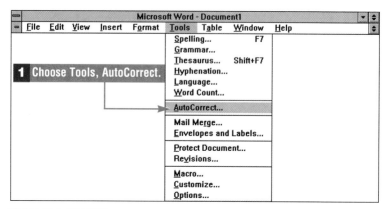

1 Choose Tools, AutoCorrect.

2 Enter a meaningful abbreviation in the Replace text box.

3 Type a word or phrase to associate with the abbreviation in the With text box.

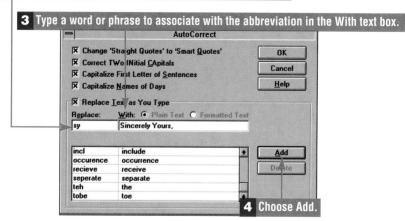

4 Choose Add.

Check any additional options you wish to be checked as you type or edit a document.

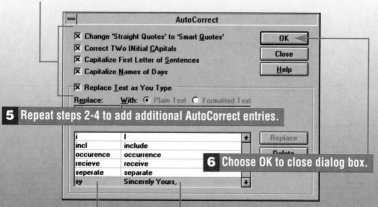

5 Repeat steps 2-4 to add additional AutoCorrect entries.

6 Choose OK to close dialog box.

Abbreviation and phrase added to AutoCorrect entries.

To use AutoCorrect

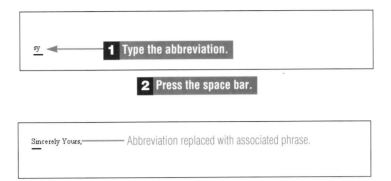

To add AutoCorrect entries during a spellcheck

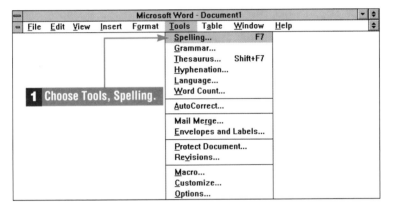

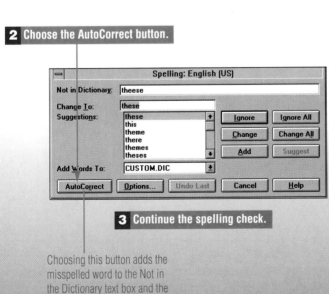

Choosing this button adds the misspelled word to the Not in the Dictionary text box and the correct spelling in the Change to Autocorrect entries list.

Working with AutoText

Word's AutoText feature allows you to insert text, graphics, and other objects into your documents. As you create and enter these items into the AutoText glossary, you assign names to the entries, and AutoText creates a list. The entries in this list are available to any of your documents.

To create an AutoText entry

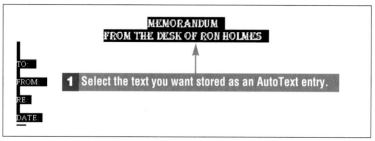

1 Select the text you want stored as an AutoText entry.

Any special formatting will become a part of the stored entry.

2 Click the Edit AutoText button on the toolbar.

3 Type a name (up to 31 characters) in the Name text box.

4 Click the Add button.

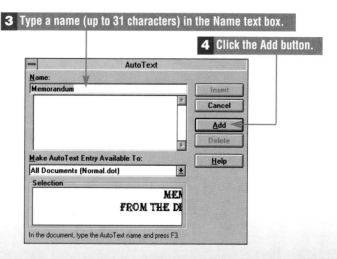

To insert an AutoText entry into a document

1 Move the insertion point to where you want the AutoText entry inserted.

Memorandum

2 Type the name of the AutoText entry.

3 Press the F3 key.

Creating an Index

Use the Index feature to mark words in your document. There are two parts to creating an index: Mark text you want referenced, and then generate the document. See "Generating Documents."

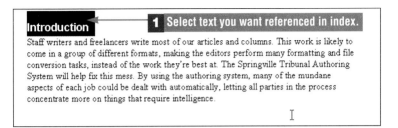

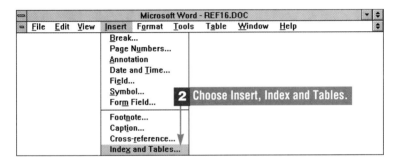

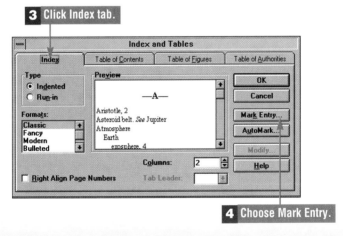

more ▶

5 Select Current Page if you want index entry to refer to current page only.

Main Entry as it will appear in index. You may edit this entry as desired.

Choose Mark All to have Word include all identical occurrences for inclusion in index.

```
┌─────────────────────────────────────────────────┐
│  ─              Mark Index Entry                 │
│                                                   │
│  Main Entry: │Introduction          │   ┌───────┐│
│                                          │ Mark  ││
│  Subentry:  │                      │   └───────┘│
│  ┌─Options──────────────────────┐  ┌───────┐   │
│  │ ○ Cross-reference: │See     │ │  │Cancel │   │
│  │ ● Current Page               │  └───────┘   │
│  │ ○ Page Range                 │  ┌───────┐   │
│  │   Bookmark: │          │ ♦│   │Mark All│   │
│  └──────────────────────────────┘  └───────┘   │
│                                     ┌───────┐   │
│  Page Number Format: ┌┐Bold ┌┐Italic│ Help  │  │
│  This dialog box stays open so that you can mark │
│  multiple index entries.           └───────┘   │
└─────────────────────────────────────────────────┘
```

Choose a Page Number Format if you like.

6 Choose Mark to mark only this entry for inclusion in index.

Text marked for inclusion in index.

`Introduction{·XE·"Introduction"·}¶`

Staff·writers·and·freelancers·write·most·of·our·articles·and·columns.·This·work·is·likely·to· come·in·a·group·of·different·formats,·making·the·editors·perform·many·formatting·and·file· conversion·tasks,·instead·of·the·work·they're·best·at.·The·Springville·Tribunal·Authoring· System·will·help·fix·this·mess.·By·using·the·authoring·system,·many·of·the·mundane· aspects·of·each·job·could·be·dealt·with·automatically,·letting·all·parties·in·the·process· concentrate·more·on·things·that·require·intelligence.¶
¶

Creating a Table of Contents

There are two parts to creating a table of contents: Mark text to appear in the table of contents, and then generate the document. See "Generating Documents."

Introduction ◄─── **1** Select text to be included in TOC.

Staff writers and freelancers write most of our articles and columns. This work is likely to come in a group of different formats, making the editors perform many formatting and file conversion tasks, instead of the work they're best at. The Springville Tribunal Authoring System will help fix this mess. By using the authoring system, many of the mundane aspects of each job could be dealt with automatically, letting all parties in the process concentrate more on things that require intelligence.

2 Click the Style button.

Microsoft Word - REF16.DOC

3 Choose the header style appropriate for your listings position in the TOC.

| Heading 1 | Times New Roman | 16 | B I U |

Default Paragraph Font
Heading 1 ─── Heading 1 is the highest level.
Heading 2
Heading 3
Normal
TOC 1   Repeat steps 1-3 until all heading styles have been applied.
TOC 2
TOC 3
TOC 4

Heading 2 is one level below Heading 1.
Heading 3 is one level below Heading 2 and two levels below Heading 1.

Cross-Referencing

Use cross-references to refer to text on a different page. This is useful because the text you are referring to may be moved to a different page as you edit. Before any cross-reference can be inserted, a style (heading, bookmark, footnote, endnote, or caption) must be applied to mark its location.

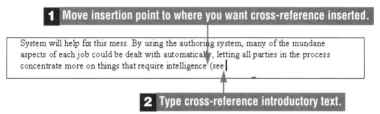

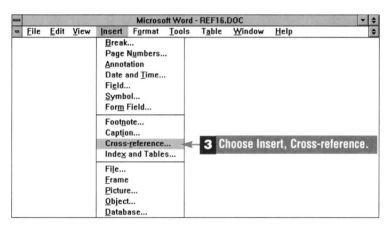

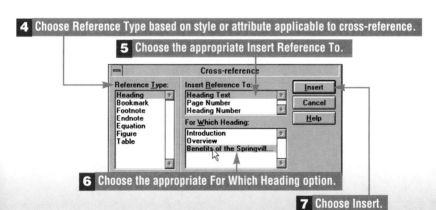

Generating Documents

If you have defined an index or table of contents in your document, you need to generate the document to place or update these items. Any time you modify a document with an index or table of contents, re-generate the index or table of contents before printing.

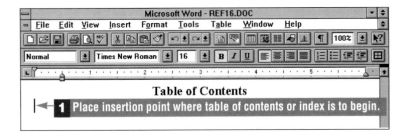

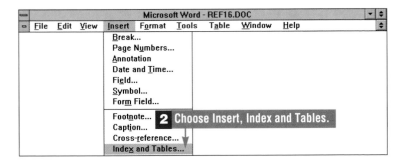

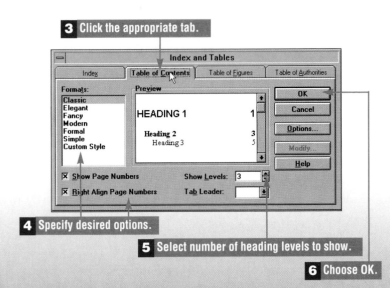

Creating a Numbered or Bulleted List

Word can automatically number lists you've typed, and update the numbers if you add or remove items. You can also use a wide variety of bullets for the lists.

To create a list

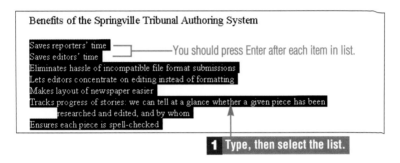

Benefits of the Springville Tribunal Authoring System

Saves reporters' time
Saves editors' time ——————You should press Enter after each item in list.
Eliminates hassle of incompatible file format submissions
Lets editors concentrate on editing instead of formatting
Makes layout of newspaper easier
Tracks progress of stories: we can tell at a glance whether a given piece has been researched and edited, and by whom
Ensures each piece is spell-checked

1 Type, then select the list.

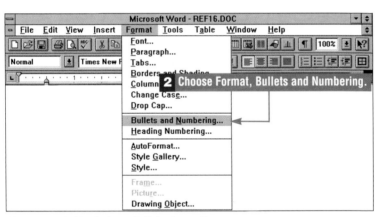

2 Choose Format, Bullets and Numbering.

You can use the Numbering or Bulleting button if you are willing to accept the default numbering or bulleting scheme.

3 Choose the Bulleted tab to see Bullet options.

Choose the Numbered tab to see Number options.

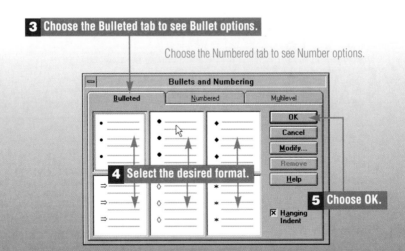

4 Select the desired format.

5 Choose OK.

137

To add items to an existing list

1 Place insertion point at the end of the line where you want item (bullet).

Benefits of the Springville Tribunal Authoring System

1) Saves reporters' time
2) Saves editors' time
3) Eliminates hassle of incompatible file format submissions
4) Lets editors concentrate on editing instead of formatting
5) |
6) Makes layout of newspaper easier
7) Tracks progress of stories: we can tell at **2** Press Enter. ven piece has been researched and edited, and by whom
8) Ensures each piece is spell-checked

3 Type new text.

New bullet entered, automatically updating bullet numbers.

To remove an item from a list

1 Select the bullet item to be deleted.

Benefits of the Springville Tribunal Authoring System

1) Saves reporters' time
2) Saves editors' time
3) Eliminates hassle of incompatible file format submissions
4) Lets editors concentrate on editing instead of formatting
5) Gives editors one less thing to complain about
6) Makes layout of newspaper easier
7) Tracks progress of stories: we can tell at a glance whether a given piece has been researched and edited, and by whom
8) Ensures each piece is spell-checked

2 Press Delete.

Unwanted bullet and associated text have been removed.

Benefits of the Springville Tribunal Authoring System

1) Saves reporters' time
2) Saves editors' time
3) Eliminates hassle of incompatible file format submissions
4) Lets editors concentrate on editing instead of formatting
5) Makes layout of newspaper easier
6) Tracks progress of stories: we can tell at a glance whether a given piece has been researched and edited, and by whom
7) Ensures each piece is spell-checked

Bullet numbers have been automatically updated to reflect deletion of bullet.

7 Click the option button to choose the type of column heading.

8 If necessary, enter the number of columns.

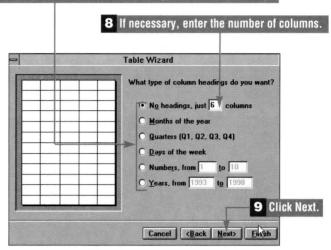

9 Click Next.

10 Click the option button to choose the type of row heading.

11 If necessary, enter the number of rows.

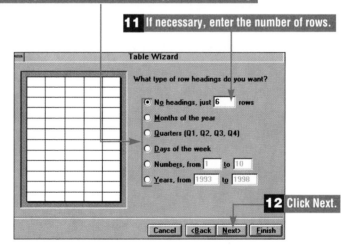

12 Click Next.

13 Click the option button that best describes the cell alignment.

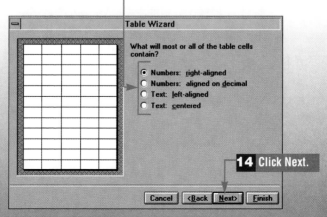

14 Click Next.

Cell alignment can be changed later, either cell-by-cell, or en masse.

15 Click one of the option buttons choose the paper orientation.

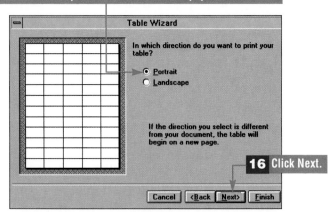

16 Click Next.

17 Choose the option button that indicates your desire to display or not to display

18 Click Finish.

19 Select a pre-defined format in the Formats list.

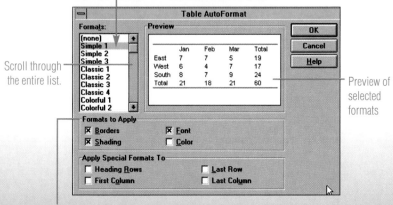

Scroll through the entire list.

Preview of selected formats

To apply on selected options, choose the parts you want formatted from the Formats to Apply options.

20 Type, edit and format table as desired.

Address	Price	Bedrooms	Bathrooms	Lot Size	Year Built
824 Charlotte Dr.	104,00	3	2	0.5 acre	1982
943 Percy St.	108,000	4	.25	0.6 acre	1990
663 Oak Circle	102,900	3	2	0.4 acre	1973
883 Copperwood Dr.	100,990	3	2.5	0.45 acre	

Creating tables using the Insert Table button

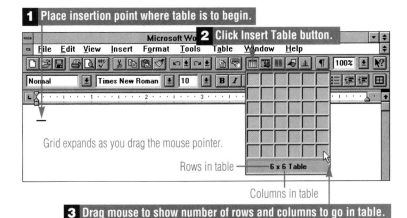

1 Place insertion point where table is to begin.

2 Click Insert Table button.

Grid expands as you drag the mouse pointer.

Rows in table — 6 x 6 Table

Columns in table

3 Drag mouse to show number of rows and columns to go in table.

4 Type, edit, and format table (See "Editing a Table"). 6 columns, 6 rows

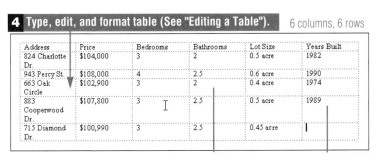

Address	Price	Bedrooms	Bathrooms	Lot Size	Years Built
824 Charlotte Dr.	$104,000	3	2	0.5 acre	1982
943 Percy St.	$108,000	4	2.5	0.6 acre	1990
663 Oak Circle	$102,900	3	2	0.4 acre	1974
883 Cooperwood Dr.	$107,800	3	2.5	0.5 acre	1989
715 Diamond Dr.	$100,990	3	2.5	0.45 acre	

Type normally in table. Boxes are called "cells."

Editing a Table

After you have created a table, you can type normally in each of the cells, as well as format the appearance of the text in the table. You can also add and remove rows and columns, change column width, and change the lines in the table.

Press Tab to move forward one cell to the right.

Press Shift+Tab to move to the previous cell.

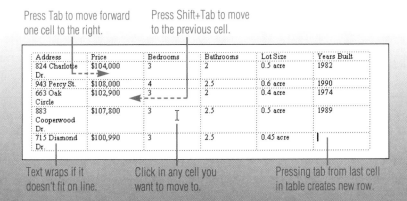

Address	Price	Bedrooms	Bathrooms	Lot Size	Years Built
824 Charlotte Dr.	$104,000	3	2	0.5 acre	1982
943 Percy St.	$108,000	4	2.5	0.6 acre	1990
663 Oak Circle	$102,900	3	2	0.4 acre	1974
883 Cooperwood Dr.	$107,800	3	2.5	0.5 acre	1989
715 Diamond Dr.	$100,990	3	2.5	0.45 acre	

Text wraps if it doesn't fit on line.

Click in any cell you want to move to.

Pressing tab from last cell in table creates new row.

To join cells together

These cells are to be merged.

To add a blank row, see "To add rows or columns to a table".

Address	Price	Bedrooms	Bathrooms	Lot Size	Years Built
824 Charlotte Dr.	$104,000	3	2	0.5 acre	1982

1 Click in the first cell you want merged.

				0.6 acre	1990
Circle				0.4 acre	1974
883 Cooperwood Dr.	$107,800	3	2.5	0.5 acre	1989
715 Diamond Dr.	$100,990	3	2.5	0.45 acre	

2 Drag to the last cell you want merged.

3 Choose Table, Merge Cells.

Microsoft Word - Document8		
File Edit View Insert Format Tools **Table** Window Help		

Insert Cells...
Delete Cells...
Merge Cells
Split Cells...

Select Row
Select Column
Select Table   Alt+Num 5

To change column width

Column is too narrow, so text in column wraps.

These columns have more than enough room.

A Short List of Homes in Your Price Range					
Presented by **Riverdale Realty**					
Address	Price	Bedrooms	Bathrooms	Lot Size	Years Built
824 Charlotte Dr.	$104,000	3	2	0.5 acre	1982
943 Percy St.	$108,000	4	2.5	0.6 acre	1990
663 Oak Circle	$102,900	3	2	0.4 acre	1974
883 Cooperwood Dr.	$107,800	3	2.5	0.5 acre	1989
715 Diamond Dr.	$100,990	3	2.5	0.45 acre	

1 Click column you want to adjust.

A Short List of Homes in Your Price Range					
Presented by					
Riverdale Realty					
Address	Price	Bedrooms	Bathrooms	Lot Size	Years Built
824 Charlotte Dr.	$104,000	3	2	0.5 acre	1982
943 Percy St.	$108,000	4	2.5	0.6 acre	1990
663 Oak Circle	$102,900	3	2	0.4 acre	1974

2 Drag column edge to new position.

883 Cooperwood Dr.	$107,800	3	2.5	0.5 acre	1989
715 Diamond Dr.	$100,990	3	2.5	0.45 acre	

Mouse pointer has different
shape when moving columns.

To change the lines in a table

1 Click in first cell to have custom line(s).

2 Drag to last cell to have custom line(s).

3 Click the Borders check box.

The Borders
toolbar is displayed.

4 Click the Bottom Border button.

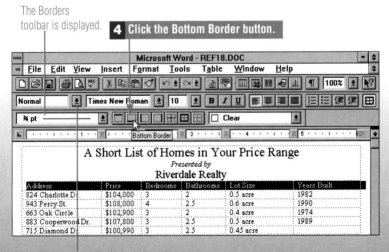

Click here to choose a different line style.

To change the table's border

1 Select the entire table.

2 Click the Line Style drop-down menu.

Click outside the selected area to deselect.

3 Click the border line style you wish to apply.

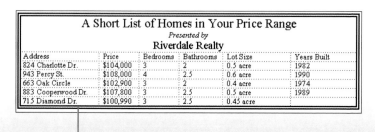

New border around table

To remove rows or columns

1 Select rows or columns to be deleted.

A Short List of Homes in Your Price Range
Presented by
Riverdale Realty

Address	Price	Bedrooms	Bathrooms	Lot Size	Years Built
824 Charlotte Dr.	$104,000	3	2	0.5 acre	1982
943 Percy St.	$108,000	4	2.5	0.6 acre	1990
663 Oak Circle	$102,900	3	2	0.4 acre	1974
883 Cooperwood Dr.	$107,800	3	2.5	0.5 acre	1989
715 Diamond Dr.	$100,990	3	2.5	0.45 acre	

These two rows are to be removed.

2 Choose Table, Delete Cells.

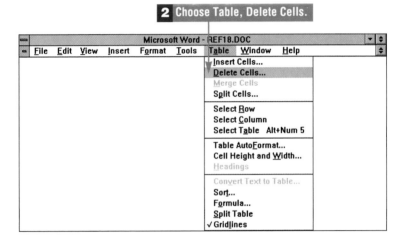

Microsoft Word - REF18.DOC

File   Edit   View   Insert   Format   Tools   Table   Window   Help

Insert Cells...
Delete Cells...
Merge Cells
Split Cells...

Select Row
Select Column
Select Table   Alt+Num 5

Table AutoFormat...
Cell Height and Width...
Headings

Convert Text to Table...
Sort...
Formula...
Split Table
√ Gridlines

3 Click the Delete Entire Row option button.

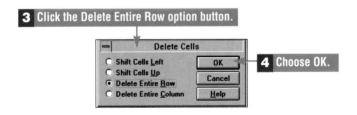

Delete Cells

○ Shift Cells Left
○ Shift Cells Up
● Delete Entire Row
○ Delete Entire Column

OK
Cancel
Help

4 Choose OK.

Two rows deleted.

A Short List of Homes in Your Price Range
Presented by
Riverdale Realty

Address	Price	Bedrooms	Bathrooms	Lot Size	Years Built
824 Charlotte Dr.	$104,000	3	2	0.5 acre	1982
943 Percy St.	$108,000	4	2.5	0.6 acre	1990
715 Diamond Dr.	$100,990	3	2.5	0.45 acre	

To add rows or columns to a table

1 Select row(s) below where inserted row(s) are to be inserted.

A Short List of Homes in Your Price Range					
Presented by					
Riverdale Realty					
Address	Price	Bedrooms	Bathrooms	Lot Size	Years Built
824 Charlotte Dr.	$104,000	3	2	0.5 acre	1982
943 Percy St.	$108,000	4	2.5	0.6 acre	1990
715 Diamond Dr.	$100,990	3	2.5	0.45 acre	

The number of rows or columns selected will be the number added.

2 Choose Table, Insert Cells.

Microsoft Word - REF18.DOC

File **Edit** **View** **Insert** **Format** **Tools** **Table** **Window** **Help**

Insert Cells...
Delete Cells...
Merge Cells
Split Cells...

Select Row
Select Column
Select Table   Alt+Num 5

Table AutoFormat...
Cell Height and Width...
Headings

Convert Text to Table...
Sort...
Formula...
Split Table
√ Gridlines

3 Choose Insert Entire Row.

Insert Cells

○ Shift Cells Right
○ Shift Cells Down
● Insert Entire Row
○ Insert Entire Column

OK   **4** Choose OK.
Cancel
Help

Two new rows added above previously selected rows.

A Short List of Homes in Your Price Range					
Presented by					
Riverdale Realty					
Address	Price	Bedrooms	Bathrooms	Lot Size	Years Built
824 Charlotte Dr.	$104,000	3	2	0.5 acre	1982
943 Percy St.	$108,000	4	2.5	0.6 acre	1990
715 Diamond Dr.	$100,990	3	2.5	0.45 acre	

Creating Charts

Use Word's Chart feature to create pie, bar, line and intersect charts. You can use these charts in your presentations and documents.

1 Select table containing data to be included in chart.

	1st Qtr	2nd Qtr	3rd Qtr	4th Qtr
North	90	50	65	85
South	50	40	45	70
East	25	30	40	20
West	10	20	30	45

If no data exists, it can be created: in chart options.

2 Click the Insert Chart button.

If an error message appears, chart may not be installed.
Run Install again and select complete installation.

3 Click here to display datasheet for editing or data entry.

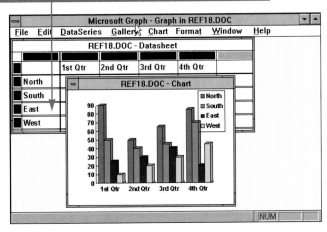

4 Enter or edit cell data.

If no data was selected in step 1, this is the place to add it.

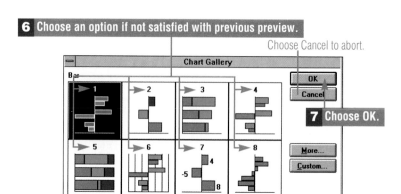

Bar Chart formats available.

Changing the Chart's Title

Put a title and subtitle in the chart to explain the chart's purpose.

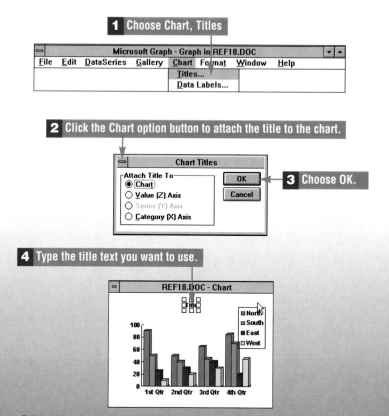

Edit the title using the normal edit functions.   Press Enter to move to a second line.

Placing the Chart in Word

When you have created a chart, return to Word, where you can size and position the chart as if it were a graphic.

1 Choose File, Exit and Return to.

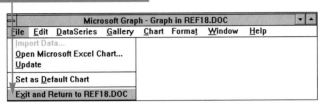

2 Choose Yes to update chart in document.

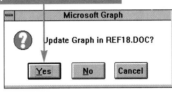

Double-click to edit chart.

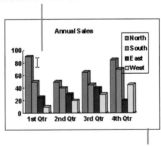

To place a table in a frame, see "Working with Frames."

See "Changing the Graphic's Size" and "Moving A Graphic" to change its size and location.

Index

Index